# Cosmic Ordering

## The Next Step

# Cosmic Ordering
## Next
### The
## Step

*The new way to shape reality
through the ancient Hawaiian technique
of Ho'oponopono*

**BARBEL AND MANFRED MOHR**

**HAY HOUSE**

Carlsbad, California • New York City • London
Sydney •Johannesburg • Vancouver • New Delhi

First published and distributed in the United Kingdom by:
Hay House UK Ltd, Astley House, 33 Notting Hill Gate, London W11 3JQ
Tel: +44 (0)20 3675 2450; Fax: +44 (0)20 3675 2451; www.hayhouse.co.uk

Published and distributed in the United States of America by:
Hay House Inc., PO Box 5100, Carlsbad, CA 92018-5100
Tel: (1) 760 431 7695 or (800) 654 5126
Fax: (1) 760 431 6948 or (800) 650 5115; www.hayhouse.com

Published and distributed in Australia by:
Hay House Australia Ltd, 18/36 Ralph St, Alexandria NSW 2015
Tel: (61) 2 9669 4299; Fax: (61) 2 9669 4144; www.hayhouse.com.au

Published and distributed in India by:
Hay House Publishers India, Muskaan Complex, Plot No.3, B-2,
Vasant Kunj, New Delhi 110 070
Tel: (91) 11 4176 1620; Fax: (91) 11 4176 1630; www.hayhouse.co.in

Distributed in Canada by:
Raincoast Books, 2440 Viking Way, Richmond, B.C. V6V 1N2
Tel: (1) 604 448 7100; Fax: (1) 604 270 7161; www.raincoast.com

The information given in this book should not be treated as a substitute for professional medical advice; always consult a medical practitioner. Any use of information in this book is at the reader's discretion and risk. Neither the authors nor the publisher can be held responsible for any loss, claim or damage arising out of the use, or misuse, of the suggestions made, the failure to take medical advice or for any material on third party websites.

A catalogue record for this book is available from the British Library.

Previously published as *Cosmic Ordering: Die neue Dimension der Realitätsgestaltung aus dem alten hawaiianischen Ho'oponopono* by KOHA-Verlag GmbH, Burgrain, 2008, ISBN 978-3-86728-060-0; Translated by: Nick Handforth. www.citylanguages.co.uk

Page 59: *A Small Boy* reprinted by permission of John Magliola © 1994 John Magliola.

ISBN 978-1-84850-121-8

# CONTENTS

# INTRODUCTION

*If one person dreams alone, it is only a dream.*
*When many people dream together,*
*it is the beginning of a new reality.*
FRIEDENSREICH HUNDERTWASSER

So what has cosmic ordering got to do with Ho'oponopono?

Just as with cosmic ordering, Ho'oponopono is based on the assumption that everything is part of a whole and that the world around us is simply a reflection of the world within us. This means somehow I have created everything that exists, otherwise it wouldn't be there. In a very similar way to cosmic ordering, with Ho'oponopono I assume the origin for every problem lies within myself and therefore the resolution can also be found within me. If I tidy up inside myself, the outside world will automatically return to order because it is only an expression of my internal energy.

Our experience over the past few years has taught us that these techniques are equivalent to 'turbo-boosted' cosmic ordering. In this book we would like to invite you to come with us on a journey of discovery into the almost unlimited world these new techniques offer. The more time we spent working with them, the more possibilities we found opening up to us. It is simply wonderful and liberating to use this method to deal with every type of problem – which even goes as far as giving us the ability to discover inside ourselves the reasons why orders have not been delivered, and to heal them.

It is only natural that sabotage programmes can sometimes occur inside us, such as *It can't be that simple!* (This doesn't necessarily have to happen, but don't be angry with yourself if it does.) This is why we have included many examples of successes in using this technique in this book, so that we can convince our rational self how well it works. The book also contains a number of different approaches to the subject, from the Hawaiian perspective to that of modern physics and current trends in psychology. One way to sum them all up, in the words of Shakespeare, is, 'there is nothing either good or bad, but thinking makes it so'.

HO'OPONOPONO means 'doing something right' or 'putting something right'. It stems from HO'O 'doing something' and PONO 'balancing out' or 'perfection'. You can also translate it as 'the path to perfection'. And 'doing' plays an important role in following this path. The more effort I put into setting things right inside, the faster they put themselves right outside.

Many little everyday problems wave the white flag of surrender after just a few 'exercises' have been tried, but regular use and repetition have amazing supplementary benefits. Once this method has become a regular routine, your inner peace creates a 'flow', a stream of life, in which an increasing number of small and larger 'miracles' can occur.

In the best cases, you begin to notice how the newly created inner energy finds its expression in the world outside and 'knowingly' begins to affect events there. You start to feel that everything is energy – and discover how this energy from the world within us expresses itself in the world around us.

# HO'OPONOPONO

*Practise forgiveness before the sun sets.*
HAWAIIAN APHORISM

About a year ago a friend forwarded an email to us, which we later received from many other people. It was an email from Jo Vitale about Dr Len and Ho'oponopono, an ancient Hawaiian technique. There wasn't really much in the email; it only said that the ancient Hawaiians believed that everything in the universe is essentially one and that everything is connected, and the effect of this is that everything visible in the outside world must also be present in every single one of us. Nothing can happen in the world around me without a resonance existing within myself.

Dr Len, a Hawaiian doctor, had apparently healed an entire ward of chronically ill patients in a psychiatric clinic, without even having met a single one of them. He had taken the individual records of each patient and, as he read them, asked himself the question, *How have I created this?*

Everything is connected and ultimately everything is one. Dr Len is part of primal creation, which gave rise to this problem – so he himself helped to create it as he is also one with primal creation; it goes without saying, doesn't it?

The email continued by describing how Dr Len spent weeks repeatedly asking himself the same question, *How have I created this?* and, as soon as he discovered a reason within himself, he said to himself, *I'm sorry, I forgive myself*, and, *I love myself*.

This finally led to all but two patients being healed in a very short space of time; they were discharged and the entire ward was closed.

Well, we believe a lot of things, Manfred and I, but this was going a bit far. Who knows if this Dr Len actually exists at all and if this could really be true? (We now know that, yes, he does exist and that he even regularly comes to seminars in Germany.) But the idea electrified us. We immediately began to try it out.

At that point in time we had nothing more than that one email, but it was enough to give us our first amazing experiences and successes. Because we had some problems with the question, 'How have I created this?' and the ideas connected to it, we developed our own methods, which eventually became:

THE DOUBLE EMPATHY TECHNIQUE
THE LOVE HEART TECHNIQUE
THE MIRACLE DIARY TECHNIQUE

The fact that both cosmic ordering and its 'turbo-boosted' version, Ho'oponopono, are founded on the belief that the world around us is a reflection of the world inside us doesn't mean for me that the individual is responsible for all of their own misery and illnesses. Nobody comes from nothingness; nobody is born into nothingness and arrives pure as the driven snow.

When our twins were born, we could tell within the first minutes after their birth that each of them had a completely different way of expressing themselves with their eyes and that they also behaved differently – and these differences remain until this day. So we clearly are not all the same when we arrive; we bring something along with us.

Neither are we born into nothingness. We are bombarded with the beliefs and opinions of our parents and families. All of the unresolved themes and feelings of our ancestors are carried forward from generation to generation through our families, and of course the society and culture into which we are born also influence us. We are what we are: a final individual product of all of these influences.

The wonderful thing is that we are all born with an innate key to freedom, at least to relative freedom. I always like to mention the Grameen Bank in Bangladesh as an example of how one can break through from rock bottom and end up leading an individual and successful life. In 2000 I made a documentary about the Grameen Bank. This bank gives loans to the poor and we were shown how, with its help, thousands of the very poorest people were able to start a completely new life. They moved up into the middle class – some of them even effectively became head of their village.[1]

The SEKEM initiative in Egypt is another impressive example of how we can free ourselves of the restrictive ideas imposed on us by our environment. In 1977 Ibrahim Abouleish bought an area of desert and cultivated it. Since then he has created an organization that serves as a guide for the future. SEKEM combines business, cultural and social institutions, which are a shining example in economic and human terms and with regard to the quality of life created. In 2002 Ibrahim Abouleish was also awarded the Right Livelihood Award (or the Alternative Nobel Prize) for his 'miracle in the desert'.[2]

So each of us carries the key to freedom within us. This key is the link connecting us to the cosmos and the knowledge that we are at one with the whole and that we can allow ourselves be supported by this wholeness.

1 If you would like to find out more, there is a free online magazine with an article about the Grameen Bank on my homepage www.baerbelmohr.de.

2 For more information about the SEKEM initiative, visit www.sekem.com.

If each of us lived our lives in accordance with this insight, then we would, I am convinced, be able to solve the majority of the problems confronted by mankind and, with each passing generation, would become healthier instead of as now, always sicker.

Ho'oponopono – or what we made out of it, as the only knowledge we had about the original techniques came from this one email – is for us a type of 'advanced cosmic ordering' because it is even more purely and clearly founded on the knowledge that nothing in our world can exist without it also existing within ourselves, and that we have within our grasp all of the tools we need to be able to heal ourselves – which then has an immediate effect in changing the world around us.

As always when I (Barbel) like doing something, it has to be easy and light. I can well imagine Ho'oponopono, in all of its forms and varieties, developing into a new party game, but one with healing properties. Until now at parties and birthdays we have always either told each other how awful everything is and how everyone around us is so stupid, or we boasted about how wonderful and clever we are and how much we have already achieved in life.

With 'hopping', as we playfully call our version of Ho'oponopono, we share our own weaknesses with each other, but in such a harmless way that it is easy to laugh about it together. However, we still achieve great depth. It is precisely its lightness, and the bond that this creates, that allow the most amazing healing of the problematic situations in life to follow.

So let's get going with a few concrete examples and detailed exercises. It's all quite easy actually, once you've got the hang of it.

# HEAL YOURSELF AND YOU HEAL THE WORLD

*I bless the present,*
*I trust in myself,*
*I expect the best.*
**HAWAIIAN AFFIRMATION**

Kirsten currently has to rely on unemployment benefit. She is working on a new project to allow her to become self-employed, but, of course, these things don't happen overnight. The only thing she has received so far in terms of assistance is a heap of problems from her case manager at the job centre, who she feels treats her 'like a piece of dirt'.

She finally came to one of Manfred's 'learn to feel with your heart' evenings and learned some of the techniques described in this book. It is all about finding resonances within yourself to all of the annoying things around you and healing them. Kirsten put her heart and soul into the exercises, and a lot of joy and energy as well. When the evening ended, all of her anger towards the job centre had dissipated – all that remained was sympathy for the difficult position of the staff who work there and the hard job they are confronted with.

The surprise and reward arrived the very next day. The job centre, which she had always needed to chase, called her up. This time her case worker, who was friendship personified, took the initiative and offered Kirsten an appointment to discuss some new suggestions of Kirsten's. Kirsten was almost bowled over when she arrived and was given a cup of coffee along with some completely new offers of support for her business idea. As she sat on her chair, still speechless, she heard her case worker say that she didn't have to come to any hasty decisions, no stress, she should take her time and think it over calmly.

'The only thing missing was the little peck on the cheek when we said goodbye,' said Kirsten with her eyes shining when she came to a follow-up evening session.

During these evening exercise sessions, I (Barbel) usually ask the group if anyone has any harmless little problem they can tell us about to start us off on the first exercise. This could be a small argument with a neighbour, colleague, relative or anything similar. In order to demonstrate the technique, it is usually easier for everyone involved if we don't jump in at the deep end straight away with highly dramatic examples, but begin with some common, everyday irritation, so that no one feels overwhelmed right at the start.

In one of these sessions, Michael told us that he had just such a problem. He designs so-called *chi* signs, energy charts to bring people success in both their private and business lives. He runs a small gallery and one of his favourite signs looks like a target. It hangs in a big window in the front of his gallery so that the children that go past it every day, over a little bridge, can't help themselves in winter from throwing snowballs at it. This annoys Michael. On the one hand, he is worried about the glass; on the other, of course, it doesn't look great for the gallery when there are bits of snowball stuck to the front window – and it's loud too.

This was exactly the right kind of problem to begin with. Everyone in the group closed their eyes and imagined that they were the schoolchildren aiming snowballs at the window and didn't care one bit that

Michael was standing behind that very same window scolding them, clearly not very happy about what they were doing.

*If I were to act like these children, why would I be doing so?* was the question that each of us asked ourselves, and *How would I feel while doing it?*

When we found a motive, or a feeling within us, we said to ourselves, *I'm sorry*, and, *I love you.* This means that we say that we love ourselves. We repeat these sentences again and again and try to experience them as intensely as possible. In this way you can keep checking whether the sentences are having any effect, or change the original feeling and original reason for acting in this way.

Afterwards we compare which motives and feelings each person discovered within themselves.

This is always the fun part! This is because it was not about trying to find out the real reasons that actually motivated the children, but rather one or more reasons within yourself. Through this, the anger inevitably transforms itself into understanding and empathy because you can understand the chain of events on an emotional level.

Rejection always leads to us cutting ourselves off from empathy. We lack understanding for others; either we get annoyed or we feel as though their actions are a personal attack on us. If, however, we immerse ourselves in empathy and understanding, this rejection disappears. We feel for the other person and we feel for ourselves. We automatically feel better and this leads to a decrease in tension in the situation, very often at the first attempt.

In Michael's case, the members of the group found the following reasons and feelings within themselves:

- If I imagine that I am behaving in this way, it could be because I feel so locked up in school, severely restricted in my need for movement. This means that I get over-excited after school and then nothing can hold me back. I have to find some way of releasing my energy. The target is the perfect solution.
- My motive would be to fit in with the group. If the others do it, so would I. The emotions I feel would be insecurity and loneliness.

- For me, it would be the chance to enjoy myself through all the activity and messing around, and also my desire to cross boundaries.
- It would be my longing for freedom – and the problem of usually not being allowed to live out this freedom.
- It would feel like an open invitation to me if someone hung a picture like that right in front of my nose. If grown-ups can be so stupid, then of course I'd enjoy it when they get annoyed.

As you can see, the motives and feelings can vary greatly, and the real reasons of the individual children don't matter at all. Emotional relief grows out of empathy. When Michael is no longer in a state of rejection and thus no longer cut off from his own feelings, then the children will feel a connection with him on a certain level – and perhaps they will change the way they behave.

- Rejection cuts the flow of energy.
- Empathy and understanding form steps on the path back towards unity.

- Unity has the power to heal the situation and to transform it.

There is also a second step to this exercise, but before I move on to it I always ask the person in question for permission before carrying it out. The aim in this second step is for everybody to feel their way into that person's share in creating the situation: 'How has he created this situation, and why?'

Michael agreed to us carrying out this second part and so everyone closed their eyes again. This time we asked ourselves the question: *If I were Michael, and I were to hang a picture of a target up at perfect throwing height, then why would I get annoyed if the children then actually used it as a target? How would I feel in doing so?*

Or very simply, *Why did I create this situation and these children's actions?* As soon as we discover something we say to ourselves again, *I'm sorry*, and, *I love you* (which means, of course, *I love myself*).

And once again the answers given by those present varied widely:

- My own need for greater vitality and liveliness

would create this situation to make me become aware of my own need.

- For me, it would be suppressed rage about the fact that I had to keep still so much as a child.
- I lack lightness of being and that's why I get annoyed.
- I want a justifiable reason for getting annoyed, so this situation suits me just fine! (This answer got the biggest laugh of the evening; everyone seemed to have had this feeling themselves before.)
- I found something very strange within me. I wanted to see what it would feel like to be attacked – within a relatively safe and harmless context.
- For me, it was the wish to be involved in more adventure. I feel oppressed by the bourgeois world that surrounds me, and the children reminded me of this.

Manfred also works a great deal with astrology. At this point he told the group that, in astrological terms, everything is also connected. The other person in this kind of situation always subconsciously feels our energy and has a tendency to express and to live out our own suppressed and unexpressed feelings for us. From an astrological perspective, we also create these conflicts because we are searching for a mirror that will reflect our unexpressed feelings and so remind us of them again.

In March 2008 I asked Michael how the rest of the winter had gone.

'No more snowballs against the window,' he reported, beaming with happiness. 'Hm...' Then it occurred to him: '... but then again, it didn't snow any more either.' We both burst out laughing. Well, that's also a solution of a kind. And next year the 'target' will surely have been sold and the next picture will seem less inviting to trigger-happy little hands.

# THE DOUBLE EMPATHY TECHNIQUE – IN FULL

*Just imagine that God is a giant*
*ball of cookie dough,*
*who suddenly has a mischievous idea,*
*born out of pure joy and high spirits.*
*He creates over a trillion cookie-cutter forms,*
*takes a sleeping tablet and with a final yawn*
*pushes the cutters down on to the dough.*
*All of the cookies tumble down to Earth to create a*
*heap of individual cookies,*
*all of which believe that they are separate*
*from one another.*
*You and I are each one of these,*
*each of us is one of God's cookies.*

Are you annoyed with someone? Does a certain situation irritate you, or have you got a grievance of some kind? Then using this technique you ask yourself the questions:

- If I were behaving like the other person, why would I be doing so?
- If I were to behave in this way, how would I feel in doing so?

And then:

- How could I have created this situation?
- How could I have drawn this grievance into my life?
- What feelings does this situation create within me?

As soon as you have found something, you say to yourself:

- I am sorry
- I forgive me
- I love you / I love me. (*You are speaking to yourself here: you love both yourself and the feeling you discover within yourself.*)

Alternatively you can also try out the following sentences and listen to your inner self to see what feels better and more intense for you:

- Instead of 'I am sorry': 'I feel with you' (*which means you feel for yourself*).
- Instead of 'I love you': 'You are loved by me' (*which means you are loved by yourself*).

Whichever sentences you choose, repeat them again and again and watch to see whether in doing so anything changes within yourself, either in your feeling or in your internal image of the situation.

You can repeat the exercise over several days – as often as you need to until the anger has permanently dissipated and is transformed into empathy and understanding or until the awful situation dissolves and is transformed.

So you have tried to imagine why you would be acting in this way, if you were the other person.

In the second step we aim to find out about our own share in creating the situation. This means that, whenever there are several people present, those who are not directly involved in the problem feel their way into the position of the person who has presented the problem. And then each person asks themselves again, *If I had created a situation such as this, why would I have done so? How would I feel in doing so?* And once again the energy is transformed through *I am sorry* and *I love you*. If you yourself are the person affected, then you also feel inside yourself and ask how you have created this problem and why. As soon as you find a reason, you say to yourself, *I am sorry*, and, *I love you*, or the alternative sentences listed above.

In the third step (which is usually no longer necessary, but is sometimes a good idea to carry out in terms of energy) the whole group asks itself how it has created this problem.

Here is an example of the three steps: Alfred reports that Bridget annoys him.

***Step 1.*** We feel our way into Bridget's position: 'If I were behaving like Bridget, why would I be doing so? How would I be feeling?'

***Step 2.*** We feel our way into Alfred's position: 'If I had created a situation like this, why would I have done so? How would I feel in doing so?'

***Step 3.*** Then we ask ourselves: *Why does this problem exist in my world, in my environment, in my practice group? How have I created it? Where is the resonance in me that causes this subject to surface at all, now that I am present? What have I got to do with it? What part do I play in it? And how do I feel about it?*

As always, we release the energy with the affirmation:

*'I am sorry… I forgive me… I love me…'*
*Or with:*
*'I feel for you (you feel for yourself; we always leave everyone else in peace)… you are loved by me (you are always addressing yourself)'.*

It was precisely this third step that Dr Len used to heal patients, whom he had not even once met personally. It is a path back into oneness: to heal 'those outside' by healing my inner self. Why do we see ourselves as being separate from all other people anyway?

Carl Jung put forward the idea that individual humans are like mountain peaks surrounded by mist. If we look down at the Alps from above when it is misty, we see each mountain peak lying singly, bathed in sunshine, but the chain of mountains remains hidden from view. Down there, in the mist, all of these mountain peaks are connected; more than that, the individual mountains rest on their chain. The mist represents the boundary to our consciousness. We perceive what lies above the mist, and are consciously aware of it. Below the mist we live our lives unconsciously and our actions are based on what is hidden. The mountain range below the veil of mist is our subconscious from which we can receive messages through dreams. Because the symbols in the dreams of all people are similar, regardless of the culture they come from, they can be interpreted and understood. Jung called the mountain range that connects all mankind, and from which we draw our dreams, the Psychoid. In this realm, all people are one.

The Sufis also recognize this mist that impedes our perception of reality. They call it the 'ten thousand veils'. The veils give us our illusion of separation and our restricted awareness. The more veils we lift, the more the reality – the oneness of all mankind – is revealed below. Then we can overcome the idea of separation and we see and feel what really lies hidden below the mist and behind the dream.

When we practice Ho'oponopono, or one of its various forms, then the mountain peak is reminded again that it is only a peak in the mist and that at its base the whole chain is one. *Every peak, every person who heals themselves, spreads this healing energy throughout the whole chain, into all other people.*

# THE HAWAIIAN VIEW

*My (Manfred's) family doctor was well over 70 years old and a bit cranky, but he still enjoyed practising medicine, so continued to treat his regular patients. He had even brought some of these, including myself, into the world. Now, when a patient came to him and said, 'My back is playing up,' or, 'My knee hurts,' or whatever, he would first reply to them benevolently, 'I have exactly the same thing.'*

When I (Manfred) hear the words 'I have the same thing,' I immediately feel comforted. 'Oh really? Well then, maybe it isn't so bad after all' is the feeling that this sentence always gives me. And I don't feel as sick any more as a result of this positive feeling.

In essence, this little story about my family doctor explains the way Ho'oponopono works in practice. Whatever I reject, for example my 'stupid' neighbour, is no longer blocked out, but rather integrated into my consciousness: *Okay, he is stupid, but so am I sometimes, in my own way.* Instead of judging and struggling against it, I become very soft. Instead of discharging all of my energy in anger or in concentrating on the problem, I consciously go into my heart and send love to the very part of me that created the problem with my neighbour. I recognize that my anger and rejection are bad for me and I choose a new path, to achieve healing for myself, improve my feelings and finally also to improve the situation.

In Dr Len's opinion, he only really works with Ho'oponopono in two ways. Using the idiom 'forewarned is forearmed', he tackles all issues he recognizes as needing attention in order to bring improvement into his life. He also sees his main task as being to 'reawaken' people who, from his point of view, have 'fallen asleep'. This attitude is also common in other cultures with a close connection to nature, such as the Columbian Koogis or the Australian Aborigines. The Australian Aborigines, for example, are intuitively able to find water and food, even in dry areas. They are still (in the sense of Dr Len and the Hawaiians) in the flow of life and in tune with their instincts. This is where Dr Len sees the second major approach for his work. For him, the only way I can reawaken unconscious or 'sleeping' people is by working on myself, on the world inside me! The maxim here is: 'Change yourself – and you change the world.'

Ho'oponopono means that I take complete responsibility for my life upon myself. I have created it, so I am no longer a victim, but can become a creator. I recognize 'You' as the mirror of myself and love this reflection. As everything is created by love, love can bring its full effect to bear through the gateway to my heart, in the loving moment of the melting and merging of I and You. The more I enter into a conscious state of love and acceptance, the more easily I can accept the problem as being of my creation and bring about change.

For the ancient Hawaiians, all problems begin with thinking, but thought alone is not the decisive factor. It is far more the continually reoccurring memories of painful experiences long past, maybe even from childhood, that influence our thinking. These unresolved issues unconsciously determine the way we think. My rational understanding can neither rewrite nor overwrite such unconscious 'programmes' as it does not know about them. It can only tackle and try to manage the problems that occur in my life as a result.

Only the level immediately above can heal and release, and this is precisely what Ho'oponopono achieves. As Einstein said, 'We can't solve problems by applying the same kind of thinking we used when we created them.'

It helps me if I love everything: my problem, my rage, absolutely everything. Love can bring its effect to bear through its inner connection to my love. For this to happen, I don't even need to know which part of me is actually involved, as love will recognize this part when I connect myself to it and ask love to 'heal this part in me'! You could also say that in this process it is the godly or higher self, or even my heart, that neutralizes and corrects the 'fault within me', as the Hawaiians call it. The negative energy, which unconsciously bound me to the old painful memory, is thereby released, as if a chain that was binding my soul had been removed. The Ho'oponopono technique can ultimately release every possible problem that can ensnare my body, soul or spirit. If I take on responsibility for it and say, *I am sorry, I love you, you are a part of me*, then the miracle begins to work. The only role that thinking plays in this is to adopt a conscious feeling of love and forgiveness.

Of course that sounds completely absurd at first, and doesn't call for a bizarre proportioning of blame. It has much more to do with examining whether all of us – if in the end everything is one – only take on different roles in order to make as many different experiences possible for each other within the game of life. At least this is how the Hawaiians see it.

I (Barbel) noticed this phenomenon recently in a member of the workers' council in a large company. The man loved to uncover scandals and deceptions within the company, both large and small. A vitally important job, as you can well imagine. I started to find something fishy about the whole business though, when news of the latest scandal reached me. He (the member of the workers' council) had discovered that a member of staff was guilty of some deception. The guilty party admitted the fact and promised never to do it again; in fact he was relieved that the matter was out in the open as it meant he no longer had to cover it up, and could turn over a new leaf.

Now you might have expected Mr Workers' Council to be happy and relieved too, not to be saddled with the problem any longer, but this wasn't the case. There was no further scandal at the time for him to uncover and that seemed to displease him at some level. He kept picking on this last man to confess, pillorying him and trying to get even more details out of him about the business, which was actually done and dusted. His manner was aggressive and demonstrated a lack of respect.

The accused could have stopped playing the game by saying, 'Yes, yes, we've been through all this already. You are right, as I told you before. I have admitted to everything and will try to do better in future. What more do you want from me?' but the guilty party was still caught up in the game, and started once again to try to hide and cover things up.

None of their colleagues could understand what kind of game the two were playing with each other – and it really seemed as if it could only be a game. Mr Workers' Council loves uncovering dark secrets and feeling like a hero in doing so. Mr Guilty, who in the end is one with him, does him a favour by playing this role for him.

Now Mr Guilty has also been placed on Earth to gain particular experiences and to play a particular game. His favourite game is hide-and-seek; this causes him stress and he then yearns for relief and release. He wants to be discovered in order to be free again.

The fact that the two of them were not looking for an actual solution can be seen in the fact that they continue to play, although the game had long since finished. Mr Workers' Council keeps trying again to uncover the secrets he has already uncovered, driving everyone in the company crazy, and Mr Guilty is trying to cover things up again, which everyone already knows about.

Each one of them has created the other so that they can play their game. Their mutual resonance with the subject attracts them to each other and has created the situation itself.

The same thing happens with therapists and patients. Therapists always attract the kinds of patients that suit them best. By supposedly healing their patients they are actually working towards healing themselves. The patients are doing them a favour by coming to them with their problems. Ultimately, when seen from the level of oneness, each has created the other.

Authors (ahem… yes, of course, we too!) always write about the thing they most want to learn about themselves and are overjoyed with each reader they find who has the same problem. For, if an author were the only person in the world struggling with this problem, then they would always only be writing for themselves. And this is exactly what he or she is essentially doing because there isn't anyone else there – only different expressions of the one and only primal consciousness. Or to put it another way, other peaks in the same chain of mountains.

So no author needs to pretend that a single line they write is written 'to save the world' or to help anyone else, other than themselves. In the end, there is always only one 'self' there: that of the whole. And we are writing for this 'whole', even if we aren't conscious of it at the time.

This is also true for therapists: if the hand writes the foot a prescription for warm socks to keep out the cold, then clearly the entire person is not feeling all that warm. Regardless of how far away the hand seems to be from the foot, they are part of the same organism and the hand essentially only pulls the sock over the foot in order to keep itself warm.

# THE SUBATOMIC VIEW

*There are two ways to live:*
*you can live as if nothing is a miracle;*
*or you can live as if everything is a miracle.*
**ALBERT EINSTEIN**

For my documentary film *Barbel Mohr's Cosmic Ordering* at the end of 2007, I interviewed Prof. Dr Hartmut Müller, Director of the Institute for Space-Energy Research in Munich, whose field of speciality is applied mathematics.

While the film crew were still looking for a suitable location, we had the chance to talk a little bit about the proposed subject of the interview. Dr Müller told me about a research programme at the Russian Academy of Sciences, which was carried out in secret for 40 years. The results didn't fit into any established physical model and therefore they initially preferred to keep them quiet. Then, in 1998, the entire 40 years of research were published at once to the stunned amazement of the scientific community.

So what's it about?

It is about the fact that protons in the nucleus of an atom always know exactly where they will fly off to when the atom decays. Each proton demonstrates a particular set of statistics, a specifically different type of behaviour from the others when, for example, the atom is subject to radioactive decay. You can tell from the behaviour of the proton during decay whether it is going to fly off towards Orion, Andromeda or wherever else.

The scientists began by observing the process of decay in alpha particles, but since then they have been able to detect the same effect in electrons in the normal flow of electric current as well.

The ability of the particles to orient themselves spatially is so clear and can be identified so precisely that it can be used for new types of global positioning systems that do not require satellites. These processes allow you to pinpoint your position to within one metre. This means, for example, in the foreseeable future, we will be able to throw the old satellite navigation systems out of our cars and replace them with new navigation systems, which work using the spatial orientation ability of protons and electrons.

Now most people don't care whether their GPS system, if they have one at all, uses a satellite or not, but the really interesting thing is that we ourselves, our entire bodies, are made up of these 'things'. The results of this research mean that every single individual atom in our body has the ability, at any one time, to pinpoint exactly where we are in the world to within one metre. It means we basically have a built-in navigation system in every cell and in every atom.

As Hartmut Müller explained, 'We humans have lost the ability to orient ourselves spatially over time. Animals are better at it. Birds, for example, can find their way south without any difficulty when it gets cold. Theoretically we should be able to do this too, as we all possess an inbuilt navigation system at subatomic level.'

Take note of this and remember it well, because a second piece of information is about to be added that gives us the perfect and comprehensive scientific explanation of how cosmic ordering actually works!

The next subject we turned to (while drinking hot chocolate in the arctic conditions of the palm house in

Schloss Nymphenburg – although we were surrounded by countless palm trees, it was still freezing cold in this annex) was: what is information?

'You can only make use of a piece of information if you can remember and repeat the thing that you have either heard or read. If you simply forget it again straight away, then the information has ceased to exist again for you personally,' continued Hartmut Müller.

Yes, that seems to make sense.

'It must be possible to repeat the information for it to remain a piece of information. This means that information only begins to exist along with the ability to save and reproduce it. Any process, which is repeated over time, is by definition a vibration. This means that every piece of information is a vibration at a certain frequency.'

Hmm… okay.

'The higher the frequency is, the more information can be stored. So what do you think? Do high frequencies occur on large scales or rather on small scales?'

Oh dear… now he is asking me to think too. So… hang on a minute, if something vibrates slowly, the frequency is low, but the waves are large and slow. The smaller the waves, the faster they travel. So the right answer must be: 'Higher frequencies produce small vibrations.'

'Precisely. And this is why only a small amount of information fits on a big vinyl record, while a smaller CD can carry a lot more and still more fits on the even tinier USB stick...'

Now the penny dropped: 'That means the largest amount of energy is stored at subatomic level in the smallest particles, the protons and electrons.'

'Exactly!' Dr Müller was satisfied; his pupil had got it.

But this is where it started to get really interesting,

Dr Müller went on to explain, 'If someone says, "Just a moment, I have to think," they are setting off processes at subatomic level. All of the neural processes, such as the mirror-neuron effect and so on, are only the result of physical processes at the quantum level. The mind can access the information contained in the particles at subatomic level, and constantly does so – whether we notice it or not. This is the crux of the problem. In actual fact, we have contact to all information contained in the entire cosmos, round the clock and without the need for anything other than our own bodies. At subatomic level, we are connected to all of the physical processes of quanta, including their non-locality.'

Non-locality means that the very smallest particles, which we and all other material are made out of, have the ability to pass every piece of information on to the rest of the universe. You are able to access this information from anywhere – if only you know how to do so. And this is the crucial point.

Based on our physical bodies, we have all the preconditions we need to be able to know everything about all of the events in the universe. But that, of course, would completely blow our minds, so we select what is important for us to know – and what isn't.

In an altered state of consciousness, we gain access to the complete store of information that exists within us in each atom. And some so-called primitive tribal cultures, and also animals, can do this without even altering their consciousness – they do it simply by wanting to know certain things.

From the point of view of a cosmic orderer, this means 'I came, I saw, I ordered' – and immediately the quantum physical processes within me started moving. Because as soon as I formulate a clear intention, each individual proton and every single electron in each of my atoms begins to search out the most fitting answer from all the information contained in the entire universe.

Are you looking for an ideal partner with 875 specific qualities? No problem, located on planet Orion 1,156 years ago, bleep. Message ends.

And we sit here complaining that he hasn't appeared yet! The universe can't do anything about it, believe me.

Remember the first part of the information from Professor Müller: we all possess an inbuilt navigation system at subatomic level.

As soon as you order anything that is possible, or already exists on Earth, all the protons within you find this information and try to guide you to where it is.

If something doesn't work out, then it isn't the fault of the universe, but rather – and this is also what I wanted to hear from Hartmut Müller – that we are not relaxed and not in sync with the flow of life force. For as soon as we are subject to any kind of stress (pressure to succeed, a feeling of insufficiency, denial of the current situation – 'this absolutely has to be delivered straight away' – and other such feelings), our whole system succumbs to this stress.

Stress, however, causes the particles to leave their individual pattern of vibration and disconnect themselves from the universal store of information. They move ever more inefficiently and, in doing so, consume more energy than necessary. Finally they are forced to start using up their own energy resources. In this condition, access to the universal fields of information is over, and subatomic navigation is impossible.

Therefore ordering in an emergency only works if you can still summon enough trust in the universe and are prepared to accept anything it delivers, whatever it is, with love. Only then will your subatomic navigation system remain active. I'm sorry, but that's just the way it is. We have all created this situation together, because we are all one, after all.

So once again – and now even with the support of a scientific explanation – pressure and stress prevent anything from working. Together with our consciousness, we are responsible for feeling comfortable with ourselves and for being in harmony with reality as it exists at the moment. Only then do the quantum processes at the subatomic level of our being function properly, and only then can we access the necessary information and let us be guided there by the voice within us.

*Take care of yourself. Take responsibility for yourself. Watch out for yourself and love yourself. Otherwise you paralyse your own personal connection to the universe. This is just the way human beings work; you simply need these basic preconditions.*

For anyone who isn't happy with this, the only option that remains is to set off after death and search for some kind of primal creator in order to complain bitterly to them when you find them. But the way I understand it, even then, you will probably only encounter another part of yourself there. In the end, you will only be complaining to yourself again, so you might as well get started now in reconciling yourself to yourself and with everything you have created. It is precisely this reconciliation with yourself that ensures that your universal navigation system performs most efficiently.

And it is precisely this reconciliation in love with all things in existence that occurs when you apply the techniques developed through Ho'oponopono – and, of course, the original version of Ho'oponopono itself.

# THE PSYCHOLOGICAL VIEW

*I am forever spared in future
the difficulties I resolve today.*

**DALAI LAMA**

Whatever I focus my attention on, I also give energy.
So it is the invisible chains of energy from my attention
that bind me to my old, unresolved and painful
memories. And this is true, although these experiences
are, of course, 'only' bubbling away below the surface
and I am not consciously aware of them. Psychologists
call this process 'repression', because something within
me has not been able to overcome the painful situation
I once experienced and therefore holds it below my
level of consciousness: my mind still wants to protect
me from the experience. This part of me really only
wants the best for me, but because this means that
I am rejecting something within me, essentially also
suppressing it out of fear of pain or simply fear of the
old experience itself, I devote a great deal of energy
to this part of me, as if from an emergency generator,

which is still running although I have no need for it at all nowadays. You could also say that in the house that is my life there are lots of little energy guzzlers that are costing me a fortune and are robbing me of energy. They cause problems for me that I can't even see because they are hidden away, deep down in the cellar.

To get a better idea of what the Hawaiians mean when they connect all of the problems that occur in our daily lives with these unresolved experiences, let us take a standard 'average person' as an example. Let's call him 'Dummy', because the way his life turns out means our example undergoes a real crash test, sooner or later. Our 'average man' gained certain experiences with adults when he was a child, mostly through his mother and father, other relatives, teachers, trainers, neighbours and so on. Some of these experiences were too painful for the child, so they weren't dealt with but remain unresolved as painful memories in the subconscious. One part of him, still connected to the child he used to be, now continues to live with the subliminal fear that a similar thing could happen to him again.

Now, if Dummy comes across a situation in life that triggers this wounded part of him, the old event is retrieved from his hard drive and he reacts to the old pain once again. Depending on the strength of the suppressed experience, his 'answer' to the situation that life throws at him can range from being aggressive to even a complete overreaction. It can often take the other people involved in the situation completely by surprise. And there we have it! A normal situation becomes explosive; it turns into a crash. The other people involved in the situation now take full advantage and judge the reaction of Dummy to be an attack or insult so that they can bring their own painful experiences into the game of life again. Of course, the unresolved parts within them also want to take part in the game. This scenario gives us an insight into what the Hawaiians call a 'dream'; the unresolved, painful part in us no longer recognizes the reality of the situation, but acts according to its old emergency programmes. Thus I act according to a protective reflex and become a victim of 'evil' circumstances, which in reality aren't all that evil. It is just that I interpret them wrongly and therefore react to them in the wrong way.

This interplay has a particularly nice effect in partnerships. The wife often becomes the screen on which the husband projects the hurt he experienced through his mother and has not yet resolved. And, of course, the husband triggers the painful memories the wife experienced through her father. In terms of the soul, this isn't such a bad idea, as the soul wants to be healed. It searches out the most likely partner, guaranteed to press all the red danger buttons the subconscious possesses. After all, these issues have to be resolved sooner or later so that the soul's energy can be freed of all of these old entanglements. The power of the unconscious in choosing a partner according to the criteria of red danger buttons should never be underestimated.

The relationship counsellor Barbara Kiesling makes this clear in a very dramatic way by asking us to 'make a list of all of the bad habits that your partners from previous relationships have had'.

*This is where you are welcome to take part!*

And now use this list to create an advert, which,

with the help of your unconscious, you placed in an invisible newspaper a long while ago. Something along the lines of the following: 'I am looking for a partner, who is totally incapable of loving me, who doesn't pay any attention to me, who cheats on me and puts me down. He should be totally unable to accept my love for him and, after a short while, should leave me again for someone else…'

Unbelievable, isn't it? But this is the exact intention you beamed out of your consciousness at some point, and this is also the precise basis of Ho'oponopono. You essentially created this partner yourself, saying this man or this woman has to be like this, in order to fit into the screenplay you are writing for your life, your inner script. Remember: behind each one of your problems lie thoughts that are drawn from an unhealed wound within you. The problem only wants to show you where your wound is so that it can be healed. This is the cosmic plan.

And this is also the good news: the Hawaiian view is that Ho'oponopono can heal all energies and problems, including even those whose deepest roots reach back to sources within our families, both on a microscopic level, as well as back in time. And the hopeful news is that the children of our new millennium will change our world, as they bring a feeling of love and acceptance with them which can hardly be shaken. 'Be as the little children, for they shall build my kingdom...'

After one workshop Ralf wrote us the following letter:

*'Dear Manfred,*
*Thank you for the very instructive time we were allowed to spend with you! On Sunday evening, we translated the things we learned in the seminar directly into real life:*
*My wife asked herself why she keeps clashing with our foster son Lukas (who is 2½ years old) although they both love each other dearly. Lukas keeps using all his might to try to get his own way, and his willpower is immensely strong! What we noticed was that, from the two of us, it was predominantly my wife who came into conflict with him. Now, based on your technique, she was aware that she attracted Lukas's rage, or rather reflected it. We asked ourselves, on the way*

*home that Saturday evening, what was causing this. Then the scales fell from our eyes, my wife had experienced a psychologically turbulent childhood, but had never talked to her parents about it. In spite of her ego, she decided to do this on Sunday evening, and it was very liberating! She told them about everything she had felt at the time, but that she had also forgiven them for it since then. Now her relationship with Lukas has finally become much more relaxed; although Lukas has not changed one little bit, the relief in tension can still clearly be felt. Thanks again for this too!'*

# SUCCESSFUL HOPPING

*A small boy*
*Looked at a star*
*And began to weep.*
*And*
*The Star said*
*Boy*
*Why are you weeping?*
*And*
*The boy said*
*You are so far away*
*I will never be able*
*To touch you*
*And*
*The star answered*
*Boy*
*If I were not already*
*In your heart*
*You would not be able*
*To see me.*

**JOHN MAGLIOLA**

A lady had a relationship with someone whom she actually would have preferred to have as a good friend. However, before she ended the relationship, she carried out some hopping exercises with him. The very next morning, he called her out of the blue and asked if she had done anything special. He had felt the evening before as if a great weight had suddenly been lifted from his shoulders.

Since then both have become good friends, and the friendship is alive and well to this day.

*'I [a participant in a workshop] work here in Berlin [the location has been changed] and am responsible for quality assurance in a technical company. Last week one of the assembly staff came to me to report a problem, saying that some of our components were malfunctioning, but that they could not locate the fault. My initial diagnosis in my phone call to the component supplier – that a very specific component on the main circuit board was defective – was not accepted. Instead of which, our supplier believed there was a different cause for the fault and*

*wanted to send me a machine for analysis. I spent the entire weekend thinking about how I could prove my theory, then in my workshop I also applied the new Ho'oponopono technique to the problem.*

*When I arrived at work on Tuesday morning, I found an email from the supplier's sales department with a product alert for the precise component in question. So my feeling was correct after all and my wish to find a way to prove it was also fulfilled immediately.'*

*'I [another workshop participant] felt hungry late at night, so had something to eat, well… rather a lot to eat actually. When I was finally lying in bed again, my stomach began to ache – which didn't surprise me, as I already knew how unhealthy it is to eat so late at night. The stomach ache was inevitable, due to my fixed beliefs. So I asked myself why I wasn't simply able to sleep well, even if I had eaten late. After all, this had never bothered me as a child. So what was causing this stomach ache right now, and why was it happening?*

*After a lot of "I am sooooo sorry," my
stomach was finally satisfied; it calmed down
and I slept wonderfully the whole night long.'*

A woman had trouble sleeping. Claudia, one of our
lecturers, explained the empathy and heart techniques
and practised them with her. This lady was then also
able to sleep soundly the very next night.

*'Dear Manfred,*
*The following thing happened to me after your
workshop, and I would like to tell you the story:*
*This year in April an assistant and deputy
head of department left the company I work in.
In addition, an important colleague had been
ill since February. When my head of department
also suddenly had to go to hospital in May,
management asked me to take over the running of
the department, all of which then went very well.*
*Then in June my boss was on holiday for
three weeks and I was expected to cover for him
and do his job. This time everything worked so
well that our director offered my boss the last two*

*days of the month off too, as everything was going so smoothly. My boss, who is the kind of person who naturally accepts responsibility for any praise and likes to blame others for every mistake, of course believed this to be a pat on the back for him. However, he didn't take the two days off but came back and started running things again, and after a few days he was asked to come and see management. When he arrived, he was asked how it was possible that while he was away everything worked so well, and since his return everything was in chaos!*

*Well, as I mentioned, he was the kind of person who liked to blame others. Since then he has been taking it out on the department and on me in particular. So after your workshop at the weekend I thought to myself, right then, look within yourself to see what his problem is and how you created it…*

*First thing on Monday morning the director asked to see him again. After a long time he came back and reported that he had just been given a good talking to. But he no longer took it out on us; on the contrary, he behaved completely normally again and even admitted responsibility for a mistake he had made. Since then the atmosphere here has been much more relaxed! So, now all I have to do is to make peace with my past, then the plan to find the lady of my dreams will surely work out... ☺ '*

A mother told me that her 13-year-old son was on a total coolness trip: his most pressing current priority in life was to ensure that he was wearing the right kind of underpants, the correct amount of which then had to stick out above his trousers so that everyone could see that he was wearing the right pants and not some kind of loser brand. For this reason, his trousers always had to hang really low on the hips, as if about to fall down completely.

By the way, I have heard this from many mothers. One of these cherished sons even takes his best friend with him to buy his underpants, to make sure that he buys the cool fashionable ones and nothing 'embarrassing'.

It is a tragic but comic fact that no one finds this fashion quite so amusing once they know where it comes from: released prisoners whose belts were removed while in prison to stop them from using the belts to hang themselves. Newly released, they then shamble around the neighbourhood without any belt, and their trousers hang down.

Anyway, this 13-year-old boy was so cool that living with him just wasn't any fun any more, so his mother applied our empathy technique. We haven't discussed the individual things that she found out in doing so, but we have talked about the results.

The first change was that the mother felt more empathy for her son and was less worried. The second was that she came across the book *Raising Boys: Why boys are different and how to help them become happy and well-balanced men* by Steve Biddulph. One of the things he writes in this book is that boys definitely need positive male role models around them (but firstly, not fathers who are constantly working, and secondly, additional mentors are needed the older the boys get), otherwise they fall prey to the disease of coolness.

Women seldom ask themselves whether they are 'real' women, but men ask themselves constantly if they are 'real' men. If they don't have suitable role models around them in their teenage years, through their lack of orientation they latch on to other orientation-less boys. Together they pretend to be cool and act as if they know everything although in reality they are completely clueless about their own identity and the direction they want to take in life.

This thesis seemed to make a lot of sense to the mother. She called up an old school friend whom she used to see about once a year and whom her son also really liked. She outlined the problem to him and asked if he would be willing to take on the role of mentoring her son and if, now and again, he would spend some time doing something with him. Luckily her old friend felt flattered and agreed to the idea straight away.

She found a second mentor in the form of a young sports trainer in a local club – and things started to change, the exaggerated coolness was a thing of the past. The trousers started to creep up a few centimetres as her darling son had found something else apart from underpants that he could identify with. And everything else changed too. He was suddenly less moody, spoke to her in a normal tone of voice, his movements became less forced and more natural, he made new friends and was much more relaxed around his mother. Finally his mother even told him about the empathy technique she had used on him.

Since then he has also been trying it out on his friends because, as he says, 'They are just so annoying at the moment.' Unfortunately I don't know what results he has achieved so far!

At the moment we have a 19-year-old boy as an au pair and he loves our sessions and all the various techniques. At one point Paul asked us to hopp his sister. She is 13 years old and so cool that even he, a 19-year-old, finds it hard to take. When he asks her how she is, she says, 'Okay,' and that is the end of the conversation.

'How was school?'

'Okay.'

'So what's new?' Ha-ha! A trick question – normally you would have to come up with more than just an 'okay', but forget it. She just shrugs her shoulders languidly and says nothing.

He felt sorry that she had been having arguments and problems with the entire family since he had come to Germany. Previously he had always been able to talk to her before she flew completely off the handle, but now her brother, the safety buffer, was missing so she just stayed silent.

So we hopped her. 'If I were that cool, why would I act this way?' and 'If I were her brother, why would I have created a sister like her?'

About a week later Paul proudly reported back to us with a wide grin that he had received a letter from his sister. She had written that she loved him and that she missed him. Wow – what a miracle! But it got even better. He had called her up and spoken to her for almost two hours. She had told him 'soooo much', and laughed and joked around with him. When his mother finally came to the phone, she asked him in complete astonishment what he had done to his sister and how he had managed it.

Then he told her about cosmic ordering and Ho'oponopono, the entire story. Now she wants to write to me and find out more.

Since then our au pair has become a very diligent hopper. Here is another success story from him. By the way, Paul comes from Ecuador and he wrote the story himself:

'Last week I took the train to the climbing centre. I love climbing. Opposite me sat a couple and I noticed something that seemed strange. The man was looking out of the window and seemed lost in thought and very serious. The woman was stroking his arm and seemed to be waiting for some kind of loving reaction from him, but he just continued to stare out of the window, wrapped up in his own thoughts.

'His behaviour reminded me of my own and that I had lost my ex-girlfriend precisely because of it. I felt within myself and asked myself, "If I were to act like this, why would I do so?"

'And I realized that part of it was pride and part of it was the wish to appear strong, both of which prevented me from expressing my feelings. What I had actually always wanted to do was to turn round to her, take her in my arms and tell her that I loved her, but my pride wouldn't allow it.

'So I said to myself, "I am sorry, I forgive me, I love me – and thank you, thank you for this realization!"

'I suddenly felt completely different, as if freed from these old restrictive feelings.

'Just a few seconds later the man opposite turned

to the woman and hugged her. I was completely lost for words and could hardly believe how powerful and effective this technique is. I could only repeat in my mind the words, "Thank you, thank you, thank you."'

Sweet, isn't it? Paul's anecdote and its effect are similar to the 'peace be with you' technique described in cosmic ordering, only that hopping is much clearer, as you are really healing yourself and not the other person. You leave the other person completely alone, and this is what makes the effect even more powerful.

Laura is a teacher. She often has to deal with pupils going through puberty in her class, who make her life pretty difficult. An 11-year-old called Markus is especially problematic. He constantly gets bored, disrupts the class and makes rude remarks, to such an extent that Laura often has to send him out into the corridor. There is just nothing else she can do.

Then she visited one of Manfred's evening seminars and tried the Ho'oponopono technique out on Markus. Whenever he became disruptive and difficult, she took the part of her that had created this problem into her heart. She used the 'Barbel technique' of double empathy to find a way into Markus and asked herself, *If I were behaving like this, why would I be doing so?* and she discovered her own boredom, an issue from her own childhood. And when she asked herself why she had created such a difficult pupil for herself, she came up with answers which mostly had to do with herself. She finally found out that this was the core reason that she herself had become a teacher.

Within a short space of time, Markus's behaviour changed. Where before he had been rebellious and wouldn't even say hello to Laura, he now came into class and shouted, 'Hello, Ms G., how are you today?' He takes part much better in class and, when he has too much energy, Laura gives him a task or lets him run around in the classroom. It is a small miracle, but in Laura's opinion it is a result of her being able to fundamentally change her attitude to Markus, as she keeps seeing herself reflected in him.

A seminar participant of ours has been divorced for many years and has two children. Her ex-husband married again, but his new wife also left him after a few years. When she heard about this, the participant sent him a text message containing just one sentence: 'Come back home.' He didn't answer the message, but the next thing he did was to write to the children and tell them that he didn't have very much free time any more and could only see them very seldom from now on.

Here's a question for you to answer along with us: 'If you were the husband and received such a message, why would you have written to the children, telling them that you no longer had very much time for them?'

The very varied answers from the group included:

- I would have felt suffocated by the sentence, 'Come back home,' and would have had to flee.
- I wouldn't have been able to stand this gift of love. I would have felt oppressed by so much generosity.
- I would have felt ashamed that I had left this woman in the first place, and would have to hide away in my great shame.
- I would act like this because I wanted to live my own life and was afraid that my ex-wife wanted to interfere.

At this point I had a question: 'It sounds as if you all share the opinion that the rejection of the children was really a rejection of his ex-wife and didn't really have anything to do with the children at all?'

Everyone in the room nodded.

'Does anyone have a different opinion?'

None of the 200 people present replied.

Then we examined the other side: 'Imagine you were the ex-wife and had sent your ex-husband a sentence like, "Come back home." Why would you have done it?'

- I was hoping to give the relationship a second chance.
- I would have written this sentence because I secretly wanted to get rid of him for good, but couldn't say it to him openly. I would have written something like this because I wanted him to break off contact with me and the children. (This statement, made by a man, caused a low murmur to ripple through the room.)
- I would have written this to him because I am still very attached to him and now, at last, want to hear

a clear yes or no from him, to finally be free again. Actually I would even be happy to get a clear no out of him so that I can finally let go.

- I would write this to him because I feel a little bit like a mother towards him, a bit superior. I would think that I knew better than him what is good for him and because I wanted to see him creep back through the front door, full of remorse.
- I would have sent him this message because I actually want to learn how to let go.
- I would have sent this message out of carelessness and would have betrayed myself in doing so: that I felt actively drawn towards his energy, the entire time.

The participant, whose problem it was, thought about the answers for a long time and came to the conclusion that a lot of them were correct. 'I wanted to make him feel ashamed; this is becoming clear to me now. And also that he wanted to be free of *me*, not the children.'

The lady had given me her telephone number so I called her up two months later, to find out if anything had changed. 'Yes – and how!' she told me happily. The door, which before had seemed to be closed forever, had opened again. It started through email contact with the children, but, in the meantime, he and she have even had relaxed conversations on the phone and the children have been over to visit him for a few days – longer than ever before.

And the lady also told me, 'I have even recently dared to ask him if he wants to take part in a school project with our oldest daughter. They need to be accompanied for four days by a father. He has never done anything like this before, but he said, "What a great idea."'

I know from a therapist friend of mine that problems between ex-partners and their children usually never have anything to do with the children themselves (especially if the children are still small), but are rather an expression of the tension between the adults. When the parents make peace with each other, are able to let go of one another completely, forgive each other and can act with respect and acceptance towards each other from a distance, most of the problems with the children usually disappear.

# EXERCISES FOR YOUR PARTICIPATION

*We can't solve problems
by applying the same kind of thinking
we used when we created them.*

**ALBERT EINSTEIN**

**As a reminder here are some of the possible sentences
you can say to yourself:**

I AM SORRY.
I FEEL FOR YOU. *(YOU EMPATHIZE WITH
YOURSELF.)*
I THANK YOU.
I ACCEPT YOU.
I FORGIVE YOU.
I AM THANKFUL THAT THE PROBLEM
EXISTS.
I AM READY TO ACCEPT THE PROBLEM AS
A GIFT.
I LOVE MYSELF.

## YOU ARE LOVED BY ME. *(YOU LOVE YOURSELF.)*

You can practise by taking part in each of the following examples.

We always start by describing the problem, and before you read the answers the others gave, feel inside yourself to see which answers surface within you. There are no right or wrong answers. Each person always finds the answer within them that best expresses the way they feel. Other people's reasons are completely unimportant. The aim is to heal whatever causes a resonance to the issue within yourself.

The act of healing always consists of saying: 'If I were to behave in this way, then I would do so because... And when I say to *myself* that I am sorry, I forgive myself, I love myself, then it changes *my* feelings in the following way.'

We never try to guess the motivations of others, but only examine our own – and heal them. We gain understanding and empathy and we heal the energy that we send out into the world. Very often this then causes a great deal to change outside, in the world around us and in the behaviour of others – but not always. Sometimes you only change yourself and stop wanting to change the other person.

In the examples that follow, it was always the case that those affected were overly strained and stressed by a certain situation or person. Through the exercises and answers, they discovered they found relief and an easing of tension for themselves and made peace with the situation in question. Once a large part of this stress had been relieved, they suddenly appeared much calmer and more relaxed.

A woman spoke about her sister, who was in the process of splitting up with her partner. Everyone knew about it already, except her partner. She was condescending towards him and ridiculed him in order to be admired for her strength by the people around her, or so it seemed.

When we asked ourselves why we might act in this way if we displayed this exact behaviour, we discovered very varied answers.

*If you want to, feel inside yourself to see what your answer would be, before you carry on and read the answers the others gave.*

Two of the answers were as follows:

- If I were to act in this way, then it would mean I hadn't been taking care of myself properly for a long time and that I would have reached the end of my tether emotionally a long time ago.
- If I were to act in this way, then I would unconsciously see my father reflected in my partner and would secretly want to revenge myself on him. I would treat my partner badly because he would symbolize my father with whom I have not yet been reconciled.

The sister was present and said that she thought that both answers were relevant to her.

One participant felt that she was being treated badly in a shop she visited regularly and couldn't understand why. After all, she was a paying customer.

The question – 'If I treated my customers badly, why would I do so?' – has always brought a wide variety of responses. One of them was as follows:

- I would do it if I felt that running my shop was too much to cope with and I got a feeling of *Help, here comes a customer actually threatening to buy something, while I can't even manage to deal with all the stupid paperwork!*

The second question was even more interesting: 'Why do I create a situation in which I feel like a nuisance as a customer?'

*Here is your chance to take part!*

Here are the answers we came up with:

- I secretly want to be disappointed. I have actually known right from the start that I would be disappointed in this shop. ('True,' said the lady in question.)
- I can't be bothered to find an alternative shop

where I would feel more comfortable, because that would mean that I would have to walk a few extra metres down the road. ('Also true,' came the comment.)

● I have a tendency to give the wrong people a chance and then expect them to change. I would actually like to learn to understand what is happening more quickly and clearly, and then to assume responsibility for myself, for example, in that I accept longer journeys or organize myself better. At the moment I still try to avoid taking responsibility for myself and just moan about how others should change. (A deep sigh from the person in question: 'Yes, this is probably most true of all...')

A lady has the sneaking feeling that her car mechanic is 'taking her for a ride' and talking her into paying for more new parts for her car than strictly necessary.

First we applied the empathy technique to the car mechanic and his supposed behaviour: 'If I were to charge my customers more than necessary, why would I do so?'

*Take part! If you were the car mechanic, why would you act in this way?*

As always, the answers were diverse:

- He takes what he thinks is owed to him but what others don't want to give him freely.
- He does it because he is under pressure from above.
- He needs more turnover, otherwise he will have to make some staff redundant.

In the second step we applied the empathy technique to the lady herself: 'If I were to create a real situation in which I was being cheated, why would I do so?'

I can't tell you all the answers we got here (this example was raised at a seminar with 500 participants, so I was only able to jot down a few responses). Some of them ran along the following lines:

- I create this situation through my general distrust of life and other people. I always receive the thing that I fear.

- I have so little myself and am just frightened that what little I have will also be taken away from me.
- I lack trust in life. If I can't see a way of proving my suspicions, I should make a conscious decision just to be happy to let the other person earn more, and trust that the money will return to me along another route.

This example from the seminar seemed almost spooky to me when, at home the next day, a plumber tried to convince me that I needed a new fitting for the kitchen sink, although only the rubber seal was worn out. He went off to get a new seal and other replacement parts that we needed for the sink. A quarter of an hour later, though, he called me from the wholesalers to tell me that there weren't any seals of that size in stock at the moment, and what should he do now?

*I know what game you are playing, sonny,* I thought to myself. *You think you are being very clever, don't you?* The car mechanic from the day before seemed to have materialized in real life for me. Perhaps I didn't say 'I'm sorry' often enough or 'I love you' and the energy was still having an effect?

Whatever the reason, it was clear to me that I had a choice: either I drive round to all the building suppliers, find a seal in the right size and repair the tap myself, or I let the lad earn his bit extra and hand the money over to him with a smile and my blessing.

I won't tell you now what I did in the end, otherwise you will think that I am just too lazy to get into my car... Well, yes, but at least I made a conscious choice and also prevented myself from sending out any bad energy along with it because, as I know full well, only I created the situation and no one else.

A woman told us that she has a friend who is compulsively late. The friend would go as far as letting her wait for a couple of hours at an underground station in town before she finally turned up.

Our first step focused on the question: 'If I never arrived on time, why would I do so?'

*Take part, take part, take part!*

The answers were:

- Purely in order to enjoy the moment. I want to be beyond the constraints of time and space, simply to be in the flow with things as they exist in that instant.
- I would never arrive on time so that I would stand out from the mass of ordinary people. It would be a kind of general, hidden protest against all the rules that exist in the world.
- I would view myself as the most important person in the world and would simply have very little respect for others. I would force them to notice me in this way, because if everyone has to wait for me, then I get a lot of attention and, though negative, the amount of energy is enormous.
- I would let myself be distracted too easily and would lose track of time. In addition, I would be so single-minded that I would have to finish anything I had started before starting anything new – even if that made me terribly late. I would simply be unable to stop doing anything I had already started.

The second question was: 'If I had a friend like this

who was permanently late, why would I have created her for myself?'

*Take part, take part, take part!*

- I myself am very punctilious and very fixed in my view of correct behaviour. I would have created her in order to force myself to become a bit more relaxed.
- I have the feeling that people who are always late have more self-confidence than those who are always on time. I would admire the gall of anyone who forced others to wait like this.
- I would be caught up in a power struggle. The person who is late indirectly takes control by making me wait. I would get involved in this struggle so that I could also take control sometimes. This actually reminds me of one of the struggles of my childhood. I think I would like to learn how to let go of the struggle and simply to look after myself.
- For me, it would be that I would want to put the other person under pressure and give them stress

with a very strict 'this can't be happening' energy.
I would put on a terribly fierce expression every
time she arrived late and let her feel clearly how
awfully she was behaving. This would create such a
strong defensive posture that this situation would
continually get worse because the other person
would unconsciously always delay their arrival even
longer out of fear of my fierce expression.

● I would have created this situation for myself in
order to learn to accept things the way they are and
to learn to look after myself better.

The person in question seemed to like the final answer
best. She decided to accept that her friend would
probably never ever be on time and she also decided
to look after herself better from now on. She therefore
agreed in future to meet her friend only at either of
their houses, so that any time spent waiting was no
longer such a problem. In exceptional cases where they
would meet elsewhere, she announced in advance that
she would only wait for 20 minutes and then leave, and
always had a plan B ready for how she could enjoy the
day alone.

Interestingly enough, after a few weeks, her friend stopped being late and since then has often even arrived at the place where they had agreed to meet before her. The lady in question put it down to the fact that she had let go emotionally and was no longer putting her friend under pressure subliminally.

In Salzburg, a participant offered us the following story to hopp:

Her boyfriend had broken up with her about 200 times already. Then a couple of days later he always called her to make up again. She had got to know him in New Zealand, where he also currently lived. Actually it was more of a telephone relationship. She didn't understand why he had ended the relationship so often already and then had always had second thoughts afterwards.

So the first question for the group was: 'If you were this friend from New Zealand and had already broken up with her 200 times, why would you have done so?'

*This is an exciting example – come on, take part!*

The seminar participants came up with the following reasons:

- I would act like this if I were caught in a dilemma. On the one hand, I would be permanently aware of the pointlessness of such a long-distance relationship; on the other, the telephone conversations would mean a lot to me.
- I would have the feeling that this telephone relationship is preventing me from finding a partner locally, but, because I am lonely, I keep calling back.
- When I say to myself and to this feeling, *I am sorry that I have created such a situation. I am sorry that it makes me feel so bad, and I love myself in spite of everything*, then suddenly my mind feels clearer. I have to either end the relationship forever or move to Germany.
- I would act like this in order to practise being independent.
- I would have a fundamental lack of trust in the relationship and in myself, and this expresses itself in all this to-ing and fro-ing.

- For me, it would simply be a familiar comfortable pattern: constantly breaking up and then making up again makes our telephone calls so wonderfully emotional. It is like an emotional adrenaline rush and much better than just telling each other what you have had for breakfast.
- I would be doing it to force her to make the final decision.
- I would ease my conscience in this way if I were cheating on her. Then if she ever accuses me in future, I could always say, 'We had broken up at the time...'

This last answer caused the entire group to burst out laughing and of course it came from a man... we all enjoyed the honesty of this answer.

Although there were 150 people present, I found the atmosphere in the group as inclusive as if we had only been 15 people and the seminar had been running for three days already. I often get this feeling when we do these kinds of exercises.

The reality is that one is always trying to make a good impression, be loved, accepted and approved of by others. To speak frankly about your weaknesses to others and in doing so to recognize yourself in others, occasionally to feel caught out – and yet still be allowed to love oneself – to be completely accepted by the group in spite of it, even to experience that the others secretly suffer from the same problems and weaknesses you do – all of this brings about an unbelievable feeling of freedom and relief. No one has to pretend to be better than they actually are any more in order to find acceptance. One can relax and be a person with light and dark sides and in spite of this, or perhaps because of this, be worth loving. If at certain stages people laugh out loud, then it is always the laughter of relief that no one is perfect and the realization that we all can find at least a little resonance within us for every other person.

Next we turned the question around: 'If I were the young lady here in this room and went along with all this, why would I do so?' And how would I have created this situation in the first place?'

*Here's your opportunity to take part again! First feel within yourself before you read on.*

- I love it when people take decisions for me, therefore I will just keep playing along forever.
- I would have a fundamental problem with decisions. This situation would be an expression of my own indecisiveness.
- So that I would not have to go through a real relationship here and now.
- Because I find starting afresh wonderful. Somehow after each time we make up I am freshly in love again.
- I would do this if I were frightened of proximity to others.
- I would be scared of finally letting go.

At the end, the lady in question spoke up, saying, 'It was incredible to hear all of these answers. It was both touching and moving. And the craziest thing is: you are all correct! Thank you!'

# HOPPING HEALTH PROBLEMS

*Love is the most effective medicine there is.*
**PARACELSUS**

A participant told us that she had had liver damage since childhood and that, in addition, she was allergic to almost all types of food and was constantly underweight. She asked herself how and why she had created such a life for herself and wanted the group to feel themselves into the situation and to make suggestions.

She told us a little more about her situation, so that we could feel our way into it and picture it better. Then we all closed our eyes and looked for resonances within ourselves.

Here are the answers from the group:

● In this situation, I would have the deepest belief within me not to feel content with the way I am and therefore feel the need to change a great deal about myself and to play doctor. In addition, I would have a lack of trust in creation and its ability to look after me and to provide me with everything I need. For this reason, I would always choose the wrong treatment.

- For me, it would be a repressed child within me that had become joyless as a result of so much pressure and things forbidden to me.
- I would have the feeling of not being able to let go and of wanting to renounce responsibility for myself.
- My main reason would be that I want to hold on tight to the familiar, regardless of how unpleasant it is.
- My wish for attention.
- The deep-rooted fear that life is a constant battle.
- My rage and anger that I no can longer feel properly express themselves in the form of this illness.
- Fear of enjoying the sweet things in life.
- The battle within me between curiosity about the new and the wish for harmony would be wearing me out.
- 'No one understands me. I am a nuisance.' These would be my aphorisms.

- The psychological pain of being unloved causes actual physical pain and illness.

Even in cases like this it is possible to carry out steps two and three in the exercise if there are several of you. The group can ask themselves: 'How have I created this problem in my environment? Why does a person with this kind of problem exist in my world and in my evening group? How can I heal my resonance so that she can also be healed?'

Unfortunately we didn't hear back from this lady as to whether things improved afterwards. But we did hear back from the next one, and the improvements here were sensational!

Frederike was at the end of her tether when she turned up at our group. Although she was actually the 'successful businesswoman' type of person, for over half a year she had been suffering from unexplained panic attacks and depression. Everything was falling apart. She couldn't work, her relationship was over and she had been turned out on the street without a roof over her head.

This was when we first met her. We (Manfred and I) let her know what we were currently working on, thinking that, since she had appeared at that moment, maybe it meant she needed exactly what we could currently offer her. You usually don't have to look very far to find the best thing available at the time.

One of these things was Dr Sha, who writes books about self-healing techniques (one of these techniques involves singing various mantras or series of numbers silently to oneself for hours). He offers remote healing sessions by telephone, in which one can participate once a week in addition to applying the self-healing techniques. This makes it easier to stay on the ball and you have the feeling that you are also getting support from outside. And it is free of charge! Which is always a good idea for someone who currently has so little money.

The second was Ho'oponopono. We were sitting in a specialist mind-body-spirit bookshop when Frederike appeared and told us her dramatic story. We quickly recruited everyone around to join in, the shop owner made us all tea and then we applied a session of Ho'oponopono to her problem.

Although she found it fascinating on that day, it didn't appear to be a breakthrough for her. She felt so helpless that she booked herself into a clinic for psychosomatic illnesses to get treatment. Unfortunately she didn't feel as supported and strengthened there as she had hoped, but more often felt under quite a lot of pressure and under constant observation by the doctors and therapists.

This is where Ho'oponopono really came into play. Whenever she was about to explode internally, because, for example, she felt she was being treated disrespectfully by the doctors, she practised Ho'oponopono by herself: *If I were this doctor, why would I talk to my patient in this way?* and *Where and when in my own life do I treat others so disrespectfully?* She discovered a whole range of answers within herself. For example, she sometimes treated her daughter with a lack of respect and very often she, Frederike, treated herself with a lack of respect. Aha – that was the nub of the problem. And that is how she met each challenge she faced in the clinic, step by step. She always looked for a resonance within herself.

The result was that both her fellow patients as well

as the doctors were very impressed. They had seldom experienced a patient who had made such great strides in only six weeks. In group sessions she was even asked what she put it down to and was asked to share her experiences with the other patients so that they could also profit from them.

'Now, of course it was clear to me,' says Frederike today, 'that I was in a traditional clinic, so I told them in a very careful and packaged way how, when examining each of my external problems, I looked for the part within me that had caused the problem to occur. In a way, you could say that I revealed a little information to them, surrounded by a safety net. And it worked. I was out of the clinic far faster that I imagined would be the case. And over time it has become clear to me that my feelings create the world around me. Each external act that I undertook out of fear pulled me down a spiral into far worse problems. Actions only lead upward when I am able to find the path back towards love within myself. Then everything resolves itself. Nowadays I can look back on my time at the clinic with thanks. After all, it was there that I was able to learn the most valuable lesson of all: that I am not as helpless as I thought I was and that I don't need any specialists to help me, but rather that only I can help myself. And I can do just that. Understanding this fact was the greatest gift I have ever received.'

Frederike also told us that she still wakes up feeling slightly depressed most mornings, and that these feelings are often too nebulous for her to know how to treat them using Ho'oponopono. But then she recites Dr Sha's mantras silently to herself for an hour, as if she were praying, after which she feels better.

Hearing this story was a wonderful confirmation for us that everyone who now comes to us for help is also unconsciously asking to know what we are currently dealing with. We don't have to rack our brains for ages to discover the most suitable thing in the world for each person. Frederike's soul already had a plan when she chose that instance to walk into the bookshop and tell us all about her problems.

# HEALING YOUR OWN PROBLEMS

*If you spend your time judging people*
*you will have no time left to love them.*

**MOTHER TERESA**

You can also apply the same techniques to yourself. Roswitha slipped into an exercise like this quite by chance. She had an employee who had been driving her crazy for half a year. She hadn't fired her for social reasons and because she felt sorry for her. But, at the most inconvenient time, this employee quit – without giving any notice at all.

Roswitha was dumbfounded. It turned out that the employee had been planning to leave all along for six months, but then on the last day she tried to put the blame on her boss.

Roswitha was already familiar with our exercises and thoroughly hopped this employee. She imagined behaving in many of the ways her employee had done, and asked herself why she would do so. While doing this she had the following interesting insights: 'I would behave strangely like this if I had a guilty conscience because I am cheating my employer: I am actually making plans behind her back to my advantage and am completely disregarding the needs of the company.'

*Aha*, thought Roswitha. *This is why she was acting so strangely for the past six months. She had to compensate for her guilty conscience.*

'Hmm...' And this was the next question that she asked: 'Why didn't I notice this earlier and instead ran around after her all the time, trying to cheer her up? I was downright afraid of her bad moods. Why?'

It is better to discuss this kind of question in a small group with people taking part in the exercise (for example, using the empathy technique), because you often have blind spots if you just do it by yourself. But the more often you use these techniques – with whomever or dealing with whatever problems – the closer you come in one way or another to your inner self. The more you practise, the easier you also find it simply to ask yourself the questions: *Why do I act in this way?* and *Why do I always feel like this in this particular situation?*

Roswitha caught herself out. She went right into the feeling of her fear of her employee's moodiness, repeatedly asking herself why, how and where this fear came from. She suddenly saw herself as a small child: she had worked out a way of surviving in life, to feel her way as intensively as possible into the shoes of her hot-tempered father in order to sense his approaching rages in time and to find shelter for herself. And since then (at that time she was only two or three years old) she had always been afraid of other people's bad moods. Now it had become clear to her and she said to herself repeatedly, *I am sorry*, and, *I love you*, to the little Roswitha from back then.

After a while, her heart grew less heavy. She even ended up laughing and giggling with joy as a released happiness spread through her. 'And do you know what?' she told me later. 'I basically have to be grateful to my ex-employee. I always believed her to be "evil" and a nuisance, but she was the catalyst for me to be able to heal this issue within me. To tell the absolute truth, I even went out of my way to go and visit three other people whose moods I have always been frightened of, and, just imagine, it didn't bother me a bit any more...'

Because she was so impressed by the success of her self-healing using this technique, the next time she caught a cold she went through her entire body in thought. Wherever she found something uncomfortable, blocked or painful, she asked the part of her body affected: *Why do you feel this way? What are you trying to tell me?*

In days gone by, she said, she would never have been able to think of an answer to these questions, but since she has been using the empathy technique and the heart technique regularly, feeling her way into herself has become second nature. It gets easier with each passing month. So now she can heal her colds in a quick and easy process by feeling her way into all of the places within her body where there are energy blockages and releasing them by repeating, 'I'm sorry,' 'I thank you,' and, 'I love you.' She only goes to sleep once her body feels light and relaxed and completely in the flow. When she wakes up again the next morning, the cold has usually disappeared completely, as she told us proudly after one lecture.

# TOO HAPPY? OH, HOW AWFUL!

*Your happiness in life
depends on the character
of your thoughts.*
MARCUS AURELIUS

A client came to us with an interesting and special problem. Her relationship was going swimmingly, her child was happy, all were healthy. The family clan was at peace, there was more than enough money about and they felt very comfortable in the house they had built for themselves.

So what was the problem, you might ask. Well, listen to the story she told us:

*'Up to now I have always had some sort of
problem and something that I can fight for or
work on. But now I have achieved everything
and this gives me a feeling of panic for no reason.
Everything is okay, yes, and now what? Where is
it all heading? I ask myself. I feel as if I am dead*

*when I don't know what direction I want to go
in or should be heading in, when everything is
already there.'*

An interesting example, don't you think? Maybe this makes it clear why you organize your life in such a way so that there is always potential for improvement. As long as some problems remain, you will always have something to do. When no problems are left, you have to learn to enjoy the pure essence of being and for some people this is much harder than poring over the usual problems. This is one of the reasons why so many millionaires are unhappy.

The aim of this client, however, wasn't to pull some new problems out of thin air, as she had often arrived at this turning point in life before and had then always created the most bizarre problems for herself and absolute chaos as soon as life became 'too good'. This time she wanted to learn how to be content with herself and the pure essence of being. This led to some interesting results that prove the following: when we feel unfulfilled, this isn't caused by someone punishing us through the current situation; no, a part of us has created this condition on purpose because it can't handle any more happiness yet.

Asking ourselves what the woman was lacking in order simply to be content with herself soon brought us to the conclusion that she was suffering from a lack of self-love.

What a stroke of luck: the techniques described in this book automatically increase the level of self-love within you, no matter what problem you are currently dealing with – through the basic fact that you examine the diversity of your own feelings and stop judging whatever comes up. Instead you say, *I am sorry*, and, *I love you* – and your level of self-love increases automatically.

We started our client off with the following question: 'Why do I create chaos the moment I am threatened with happiness? Why do I slam the door in the face of happiness?'

We closed our eyes, everyone present joined in. Our client then had a vision where she could see happiness shining bright in front of her, but between her and her happiness there was a mound of rubbish blocking her way. It wasn't possible just to make a detour around the mound; wherever she went it just moved in front of her.

Hmm, what should she do? In her thoughts, she simply said to the mound of rubbish, 'I thank you for being there,' and, 'I love you.'

Now something amazing happened: the mound of rubbish moved to one side by itself and freed the path to her happiness.

Just then, the lady had a little moment of epiphany. Up to that point she had always tried to erase the uncomfortable part of herself. She wanted to get rid of it and destroy it. She had used avoidance strategies, so that the mound grew ever more threatening. Though now she found she could also love this part of herself and accept it completely as it was, the part felt satisfied. It didn't disappear, but moved out of the way. Only by accepting the part of her that was rubbish was she able to choose her brighter side. In doing this she had discovered a deep truth about herself: the things we suppress impose themselves on us ever more until we simply accept them for what they are. Only then are we free to choose again.

A different participant in the group, who had taken part as well, had also imagined that happiness had knocked on his door and that he had slammed the door in its face. He became very sad and asked himself, 'What would be my reason for acting in this way?' His answer was, 'A part of me is frightened that the essence of myself would disappear if I were to experience unbounded happiness.'

Also very interesting, don't you think?

But we were far from finished. The next thing our ambitious client wanted to know was why she couldn't unconditionally and completely love and accept herself the way she is.

Once again everyone closed their eyes and we felt within ourselves by asking the question, *Why don't I love myself completely and simply the way I am?* (As everyone was already familiar with this problem, we could all just ask the question directly.)

*Do you want to take part?*

The first answer came from the client herself:

*'I would be scared that – if I loved myself
completely the way I am – I would also love
everything around me as it was as well. Then
I wouldn't be able to judge anything that I
encountered any more. But this would also mean
that I would lose my protection and the ability
to navigate at this level of being. Just being
surrounded by love has given me the feeling of
being vulnerable. And as I said to myself, 'I
thank you,' and, 'I love you,' I was suddenly full
of joy. Until now I had always thought I was
simply too stupid to love myself completely. But
now I think that I am doing exactly the right
thing and doing it well enough to be secure in
this world. And – abracadabra – I love myself
much more than I did before because I have
stopped judging myself for my lack of self-love.'*

Wonderful, don't you think? No movie in the world
could be as interesting as the emotions we discover
within ourselves about our most secret motivations.
And these vary from person to person.

Another participant in the group found a completely different answer:

> *'I only had the feeling that I would only be able to experience a life on Earth at all through the separation from the all-loving essence and with a minimum of self-doubt. If I were pure love, it would simply beam me away from this level of consciousness. Given this, a certain well-measured dose of self-doubt would be my entrance ticket, allowing me to live an earthly life.'*

Even this is a feeling that everyone must feel sometimes. But it is a feeling this participant uses to create his reality.

# OVERVIEW OF THE
# SELF-HEALING TECHNIQUES

1.  Self-healing, when carried out in this way, works all the better the more often you practise the basic techniques, regardless of the issue involved. You see the hidden motives for your feelings more clearly in the light of day and they become more trusted and familiar to you. Your sensitivity towards yourself becomes ever finer.

2.  The essence of each of these techniques is self-healing because it is all about the resonance within you towards the things you are healing. But also very concrete issues you have with yourself can be dealt with directly.

3.  If you notice an aspect of your behaviour that does not seem ideal to you, ask yourself why you are doing it. Why have you created this pattern of behaviour for yourself? And when you find any

reason for it, no matter whether it seems logical, absurd, funny, understandable or not, say to yourself, *I am sorry*, and, *I love you* (or another sentence from the basic list, according to what feels best at the time).

4.  If you feel bad in a certain situation, also ask yourself why you have created this feeling. And say one of the releasing sentences to yourself.

5.  Take both your behaviour and the unloved feeling into your heart and say to them, *You are also a part of me. I haven't been able to prevent you up to now, so from now on I will consciously allow you to be a part of me. I love you – and me with you – exactly the way I am.* Imagine with every breath you take that your heart is getting bigger and bigger, so that all of your behaviour patterns and feelings find room within it. When you breathe out, allow your heart to return to its normal size.

6.  You can follow the same procedure for individual organs or parts of your body that are currently

not doing so well. Ask the part of your body in question, *Why do you feel this way? How have I created this feeling?* and each time you discover an intuitive idea or feeling, say once again, *I am sorry... I love you.*

7.  You can carry out these exercises by yourself and take notes. Repeat them again on as many consecutive evenings or days as you need until you feel completely restored and liberated, or until you can no longer detect any resonances within yourself towards the issues.

8.  You can also invite friends round on a second evening (or day) and ask them to feel their way into the problem and to let you know what ideas they discover in doing so. Maybe you will receive additional valuable insights from them if you describe, for example, that you always get a tense feeling in your stomach and ask yourself how you have created it. When you then practise the heart technique with each other, the feelings often go far deeper than when you practise it alone.

# THE HEART TECHNIQUE

*Those who only look out, dream.*
*Those who turn within themselves, wake.*

CARL JUNG

In private, we also call the heart technique the 'Manfred technique' because Manfred likes to work with this technique best, whereas Barbel prefers double empathy.

The heart technique is fairly fundamental and in essence very simple. Whatever your problem is, you only need to take it into your heart and to say:

*'Whatever has caused this problem, it must have something to do with me.*
*I love the part within me that has caused the problem, I accept it fully. I forgive this part of me, I thank this part of me.*
*I give this part of me all my love.'*

I (Manfred) repeat this procedure until the problem disappears into thin air. And, above all, I immerse myself fully in the feeling of love to detect which feeling is revealed through this meditation and exercise. Then I also explore this feeling and give it all of my love. And that's it. There is very little you need to know in order to do this, but a lot that needs to be felt.

It is also very effective to repeat the following throughout the day like a mantra: 'I love, I love. I love this and I love that. I love everything that happens to me. I love my problem.' This is a variant on Barbel's 'peace be with you' cosmic ordering tip.

At some point many years ago the moment came when it became clear to me that accepting the truth is the most important thing in the world. And Ho'oponopono really makes it very easy: I have created 'it', so I can also change 'it'. However, the key questions here are: *How do I enter into the feeling of love? How do I reach the heart?* The further I delve into my heart, the stronger the effect of the technique. And, of course, then my cosmic ordering also works best. This is exactly why we view these techniques as advanced cosmic ordering as they require the willingness to really look within and to form and nurture the contact with your own heart.

In essence you can use any method you like to do this. You can meditate. You can sing. You can light a candle in your heart or lay hands on your heart. You can do it by yourself or in a group. And, of course, you are welcome to come to one of our seminars, as any exercises that help you feel and experience are a very important element in all of the techniques.

A note from Barbel: when Manfred runs workshops by himself, then feeling is more central; when I run workshops by myself the focus is more on the double empathy technique.

Another important thing: a short time ago we held a 'life happiness' seminar where I (Manfred) explained the heart technique. A man at the front became very agitated, saying, 'I can't do this, I have no idea how I am supposed to enter my heart. I probably have to practise a lot more until I can manage to do it even just a little bit.'

Evidence once again of the 'blockage' within us, which makes us think, *Don't even bother trying, of course you can't do it. Just leave it be, then you won't be disappointed.* When I worry that *I just can't do it, I will never be able to do it, I will have to go to another ten courses first, I always need someone to help me,* and so on, then that sentiment will always actually be true in my world. I won't even give the heart technique a try because, of course, I can't do it yet. At least that's what I believe.

But there is help for the poor chap. It is certainly true: the more I am in my heart, the better the technique works, because then the power is stronger. But it also works just fine before I even have a clue about what it means to be in my heart. It works very well without any energy from the heart – because in principle it suffices if you release yourself from the energy of rejection. So put a stop to your struggle and resistance.

If I swing back to the 'zero position', where I neither love nor fight, I will have already reached the field of unimagined possibilities. The thing in my life that creates the most problems is rejection: the struggle, being opposed to things. My battle-hungry energy creates external problems. If I manage to end my rejection with the sentence 'I love that part of me that causes the problem,' then anything can be possible. This is enough to cause a transformation.

Why is this so? In my opinion it stems from the fact that love is always there in any case, even at the zero position. Love always has an effect – or would have an effect if I allowed it to… When I reject and struggle against it, the heart technique unfortunately doesn't work, because then I am fighting against that which is. However, 'that which is' is always 'somehow' love, even when it seems hard to believe and also when it is difficult to recognize it at times.

For me, the heart technique in particular opens up a new horizon and offers an often incredible perspective on things. This fact alone can achieve a great deal.

One evening, Rita, from my practice group in Munich, was working on the issue of her father. Up to that point she had been conscious of the fact her whole life long that her father didn't love her and that she hadn't received enough attention from him. After hopping and working with the heart on her issue, she was very quiet and hardly wanted to say anything about what she had discovered. Finally she told us: she felt that everything had changed! She suddenly realized that her father had been seeking a lot of love from her, his little girl – love that he himself had never received from his parents. In secret he was still a little child searching for love.

# THE LOVE TECHNIQUE

*You and I are one.*
*I cannot hurt you without harming myself.*
MAHATMA GANDHI

*You haven't discovered the truth if it*
*doesn't increase love.*
*What's more: only love exists, or the cry for love.*

The love technique combines both the heart and mind. If you have applied the double empathy and the heart technique to someone you are angry with, but are somehow still angry when you think of them, then it is time to try the love technique.

Think about the behaviour that annoys you most about the other person and ask yourself whether it might possibly be an expression of love: *What does the other person love, when they act in this way? What are they defending, maybe unconsciously, through their actions?*

Or if it probably is not an expression of love, or at least if you can't imagine it, could it possibly be a cry for love? How do you feel if you view each expression of non-love as a cry for love? How could you decently ignore this perhaps desperate and totally unconscious cry for love?

A participant in one mini-group told us in the session about a business competitor who had been causing him problems wherever possible for almost ten years now. The double empathy technique only satisfied him to a certain extent: while he could imagine the motives of the other person, it didn't significantly diminish his feeling of anger towards him. The frustration just ran too deep.

So we tried it with a cry for love: 'Imagine that the behaviour of your competitor were a hidden cry for love.'

Complete bafflement. He felt inside himself for a few moments and didn't say a word. Then suddenly he began to grin: 'If I imagine that it is a cry for love, then my fear of him collapses like a house of cards. I think, after all, that my anger is only an expression of the fact that I feel threatened by his behaviour and am frightened of him. If it is a cry for love, then *he* is the weak one, not me. That would change everything.'

We all thought together about how we could answer this cry for love objectively for our acquaintance. We wrote a script together and the next day he called his competitor on the phone. He explained to him that he had a small problem in his company, and pretended that he had no idea how to handle it. He continued, saying that he had heard that his competitor had absolutely no problems with this issue in his firm, and that his staff seemed to be very contented and asked him if he had any advice.

At first it was his competitor's turn to be completely baffled, but then he started talking. He lectured his 'adversary' on the phone for over an hour. He finally received praise and recognition from him, so, in a certain respect, also love. He showered his competitor with a waterfall of words, almost like a blessing.

Since then everything has been quiet and the two companies now exist as peaceful neighbours.

# THE MIRACLE DIARY TECHNIQUE

*Most people take a long time
to become young.*

**PICASSO**

The miracle diary technique came about when I (Manfred) was trying to heal the fear of a future event in advance.

It is generally agreed by everyone that decisions and actions taken as a result of panic and fear mostly lead to even more chaos and drama. The decisive factor in the success or failure of anything I undertake is the energy in which I do it. This is true for a wish as much as for a concrete action. If I do something in the firm belief that 'it is never going to work', then this result will surely follow. If I do something in confidence and power, then I am much more likely to succeed. Henry Ford put this in a nutshell: 'Whether you believe you can do it or you can't – you are right!'

I had been commissioned to give a company seminar on positive thinking in Dresden. The manager of a small car company wanted to give her staff 'a treat'. She had been involved in esoteric issues for a long while and thought it was about time to improve the general negative attitude in the company a little.

Many employees viewed the suggestion as enforced happiness. There were whispered conversations in the corridors about brainwashing and Scientology until, shortly before the chosen date, open criticism broke out, which the manager only managed to contain with difficulty. Two days before the date she asked me if I was still prepared to hold the seminar under these circumstances. Screwing up my courage, I said yes.

On the drive to Dresden I had to deal with all of my fears and doubts. I kept having panicked thoughts about the staff tarring and feathering me, or that at best they would just sit there silently, that many would not come at all, and those that did would probably decide to go home again at once.

As soon as a feeling of fear and inability rose within me during the drive, I healed it with the words, 'Dear feeling, I love you, I accept you, you also have a right to exist.' And to myself I said, *Come on, old boy, just calm down a bit! If you turn up surrounded by this energy, you know exactly what is going to happen.* I talked myself out of my delusions as you would a small child.

And it really did work: all of them stayed. Even the biggest troublemaker admitted at the end that 'it wasn't all that bad'. And there was never the smallest indication that open warfare was about to break out.

I also have to admit that I had more negative feelings along the lines of *They won't pay the invoice; they will only pay part of it, or take months to pay it because they will all be so unsatisfied.* But I also worked intensely with these feelings on the journey there. And, lo and behold, the seminar had barely finished before the manager started counting the banknotes out in front of me...

A man who came to one of our groups had a problem with one of his relatives. This relative, he told us, 'can't manage to do anything right, jobwise'. Instead he would launch into a barrage of prevarications and excuses at each family event about how everything was so difficult, nothing was possible and so on and so forth. There was neither rhyme nor reason to anything he said; he was so overblown with self-importance, completely unconstructive and very tiring to listen to. The man in our seminar felt intensely irritated by it all and was already worried about the obligatory Christmas get-together that was looming.

The other participants, on the other hand, were fascinated. It sounded like an interesting case to feel their way into and empathize with. The more often you use these techniques, the more you notice how, bit by bit, you delve into the depths within you and explore them, without experiencing any danger, and can examine them from all perspectives and then heal them. So they thought, bring on the weird guy! Let us find our own part in him and heal it!

In answer to the question we asked ourselves, 'If I were to release a barrage of prevarications, without rhyme or reason, why would I do so?' we discovered the following reasons:

- For me, it would feel as if I no longer had my feet on the ground. I would only be living in my imaginary world and would no longer be able to properly assess the real world around me.

- If I were to act like this, I would do so to escape from the present. It is too painful to look at the truth openly. This is why I would retreat in panic into my castles in the air.
- I would be separated from my real feelings and would not be able to feel myself any more. This is why my entire life is so unclear. I would talk this much in the hope that it would help me to sort myself out a little internally.
- I might do this if I defined myself purely through ingenuity and great ideas and if I had the fundamental feeling that 'carrying my plans out is actually not necessary once I have given such wonderful lectures on the subject'.
- I might be speaking wildly and without any real plan if I were frightened of having to take definite decisions. Whenever I am tortured by the worry of taking the wrong decision, I therefore would not take any at all, but just weigh up everything for ever in my mind instead.

After we had listened to all these different answers in amazement, we moved on to step two of the technique and asked ourselves, 'If I had created such a long-winded person in my life, why would I have done so?'

And these were the results:

- Because, looking on the bright side, he (the pain in the neck) is always willing to listen to the crazy ideas of others and he is a good person to talk through new ideas with.
- I would have created him to make myself feel better. To be able to think, *Now just look at him jabbering away, desperate to get some recognition. What luck I have that I am better than him.* But I think, when I look at it like this, that this doesn't give me any right to speak badly about him, I have to admit that on some occasions I also like to do this too...
- I think that my soul wants to learn to be in love, even in a situation like this, because, after all, I also have an arrogant part in me that wants to feel superior. (This is the reason the person in question himself gave!)
- I would create something like this for myself if I

had the compulsive tendency to look for a rational solution to every problem.

The statement of the last participant created a general buzz of amusement.

'What do you mean by that?' the others wanted to know.

'Well, I would instead want to practise going into the feeling of trust, to make a nice and harmonious evening possible in spite of everything, so that I could be the one that creates it. Rational arguments are often useless in dealing with such people. But if you form a clear intention in love, and trust in cosmic help, then it is possible...'

General astonishment – and the right time to explain the 'miracle diary' to this group too. Because this is exactly what you do with the miracle diary: positively influence situations in a non-rational way.

In the case of the man with the long-winded relative, he could write everything that he wanted to happen down in his diary the evening before the event. This means to start with, you visualize the atmosphere that you would like to have for the evening and you imagine that the evening goes so harmoniously and cheerfully that everyone present without exception – including yourself – enjoys it.

Well, you may have one or two not quite so positive expectations of the evening. So you ask yourself, *What obstacles could arise and how would I feel if they do so?*

And then you take these obstacles and feelings into your heart, through your thoughts, and say to yourself, *I'm sorry*, and, *I love you.* You can also be very concrete: *I am sorry that you are so frightened of the torrent of words from What'shisname. I am sorry that you feel so uncomfortable about it. I love you. I am sorry.*

In doing so you heal the resonance you have to the situation before it takes effect and so you allow it to take a new direction.

In the case of the long-winded relative, the next evening with him not only went better but was completely different. The conversations were comprehensible and thought through – completely the opposite of how they had previously been.

And a funny detail, in answer to the question of why he had created this relative, the man affected had, among other things, found out that he wanted to learn how to overcome his feeling of superiority towards him!

A few days later, a colleague confessed to him that he had the feeling that he sometimes acted stupidly towards other staff because of his own feeling of superiority. He wanted to remedy this. It seemed to our man in question that revelations were infectious...

# VARIOUS AREAS OF APPLICATION

*Shadows I reject*
*return to me as fate.*
CARL JUNG

As enthusiastic cosmic orderers, we see ourselves as co-creators and devisers of our own reality. It will never be possible to do everything, but we want to fully exploit our potential instead of allowing ourselves to be overtaken by the unresolved feelings of our ancestors or of our own childhood. The techniques presented here enable us to deal with everything that still causes us problems. We erase the *fait accompli* described by Carl Jung, a predestined fate that grows out of our repressed shadow side, and replace it with a fate *à faire*, which we can form and control.

And the secret is that we can have a lot of fun in doing so. Deep-seated revelations are, at times, coupled with much laughter and bonding within the group. They can be accompanied by lightness and simplicity.

Maybe you have already gained a 'taste' for it and can see a new, positive and healing party game in these techniques, particularly the double empathy technique. Hopping is clearly more of a game than work, more fun than sad and more light than heavy.

Also, if tears sometimes flow and long-forgotten pain returns briefly, they are taken into the heart, allowed to exist, allowed to be felt and allowed to depart again. This often happens very quickly, as hopping is not a long-drawn-out technique. Instead the desired aim is a quick feel around inside and exchange of the varied views of the participants.

At that instant we are grateful for each problem we hopp, so that we can 'keep on playing'. In order that you don't run out of game possibilities, what follows below is a list of areas to which you can apply all of the techniques we have described.

It is clear that I (Manfred) find the most important playground for hopping in my close interpersonal relationships. This, of course, is where the projection of my spiritual side on to others works best, and this is also where most people push my red danger buttons. Have you ever noticed that children are always perfectly well behaved at their grandmother's, but occasionally cross the boundary of 'liveliness' at home? (I love the part of me that has created this…!). This is also one of the main tasks in my environment: to trample around on my ideals and unresolved issues so that I can release them. The unfortunate thing is that Barbel and I can't even argue properly any more since we found out about hopping. These kinds of discussions usually end up with, 'Okay, I love the part of me that created this pain in the neck,' or, 'I forgive myself for creating a pattern where someone always does this or that…!' With these kinds of sentences you can only have fights for entertainment, but then you still have to laugh when you have them anyway.

You can ask yourself the following questions when you feel like a round of hopping:

- Whom do you repeatedly have problems with?
- Whom don't you feel completely comfortable with?
- Whom do you have the feeling with that he or she is using you, regularly takes you for a ride, goes over your head, speaks badly about you, etc.?

Which relationships can still be improved? My relationship with my...

- colleagues
- employees
- boss
- business partner
- partner
- children
- relatives
- friends or ex-friends
- neighbours (but only if you really want to – think about it carefully! We received a complaint by email from a woman who hopped her neighbour. This person has been breathing down her neck ever since and chosen her to be her favourite neighbour. This was not the plan at all; she had only wanted to find a peaceful way of getting rid of an annoying neighbour...)?

If orders are not delivered, then the reason for this also lies with me. This is also a problem I can hopp. I can aim for improvement here too. Of course, I usually have no idea exactly *why* an order does not get delivered, but the genius of it is that I don't even need to know why. I simply go into my heart and take the part that has created the blockage to the delivery into my heart and love it. This works, for example, for an unfulfilled wish to have children; I love the part of me that is preventing me from getting pregnant and accept it completely.

I can also take the thing preventing my wish from being fulfilled 'generally' into my heart, without knowing who or what it is exactly.

In small groups, however, it is also very revealing and fun to use the double empathy technique on the issue: 'If I were the part of X or Y that was preventing the wish from being delivered, why would I do so?'

Bertram, for example, had placed an order that he would finally be able to become self-employed – but it just wouldn't seem to happen. We hopped the things preventing the delivery, and what do you think was revealed?

● If I were the part preventing the delivery, then I would be frightened of responsibility. It is so much more secure to be an employee.

- I would be scared of giving up my comfortable life and possibly really having to get down to some seriously hard work.
- I love daydreaming about my ideal job. I would prevent the delivery because I would want to keep on dreaming in peace instead of having to deal with the irritations of putting it all into actual practice. As long as it is just a dream, I don't have to look for any employees, fill out any tax returns or rent an office.
- The preventer within me says that if you really want something, then you will also get it. But I first have to convince the blocker that I am being absolutely serious about this wish and that I am also prepared to bear the consequences.

We took all of these different preventative factors into our hearts, accepted them completely and gave them our love: *It is okay that you are here and that you are what you are.*

Bertram said that this had completely freed him of the things he had always accused himself of until then. Right now, he has a permanent job three days a week and is partly self-employed – completely free of any stress and pressure. He had been convinced before that it would have to be all or nothing.

The ancient Hawaiians believed that the rule 'Whatever happens on Earth must also be present within you' applied to everything. Even for terrorism (both in terms of the terrorists and the government), wars, illnesses, violence, suppression, environmental pollution, exploitation and so on and so forth.

This means that you can hopp everything that affects you and that you want to improve. The wonderful thing about hopping is that you do not interfere in the lives of others in applying it, but remain completely within yourself.

Even for a war in a far-off country, the question would be, *How have I created this thing so that it exists in my world? How can I take it into my heart? I am sorry and I love myself.*

*You do not love the warmongers, nor do you love the victims. You love that part within yourself that has a resonance to it. If we were to heal the resonance to war within us completely, then wars would have to cease to exist in the world.*

I find this insightful. Let's take food production as an example. People regularly complain about poor quality or even about polluted food and then the producers are scolded, as if they were to blame. But in my opinion everyone who always insists on buying the cheapest food possible actually shares in the responsibility. This behaviour increases the turnover of the discount producers and reduces that of the quality food producers.

And if everything has to be dirt cheap so that consumers will buy a product, then you can't ensure that the animals going to slaughter are fed healthily or that the equipment used in production is cleaned biologically, without the use of chemical detergents.

The business accused has to manufacture its product as cheaply as possible in order to earn at least something in the process. If the majority of consumers chose only quality products and elected to buy more expensive items, such as meat, less often and instead to eat more rice or good-quality vegetables, then the same producer would probably start an organic chicken farm to meet the needs of the consumer.

This is how your own internal behaviour helps to create these problems, even if you are not a food producer yourself. I have been preoccupied with this subject because I recently saw the film *We Feed the World* on DVD.[3] This film demonstrates how consumer purchasing behaviour influences the production of fish, meat and even vegetables. It shows how the fact that hens can be raised without even getting to see the sun for a single day is not the fault of the producer but the result of consumer behaviour, as free-range hens simply can't be raised that cheaply. But it is even trickier than that. As a consumer of organic food, I live in a world where genetically modified seeds can blow over from a neighbouring farmer's field. How did I create a situation where I can't enjoy my natural organic food in peace? An interesting question. We can hopp it together at the next seminar.

3 Visit www.we-feed-the-world.at – in spite of its title, the film is in German.

I only want to say that you can hopp everything, make peace internally with it and, on an energy level, contribute to improving it.

I (Manfred) used to work in an office, where there was a photocopier in the corridor that was used by the whole department. My little office was right next to it. Every Monday morning, a nervous, stressed woman rushed over to it with a mountain of papers, which urgently needed to be copied. And the copier broke down. Every single time! Now this woman was such a bundle of nerves that her anxiety transferred itself to the copier. This put her into an even worse state than before and she would invariably beg me for help. I used to send her off to get a cup of coffee and basically 'laid my hand' on the copier. I always tried to approach it very calmly and asked, 'Well now, what's wrong with you?' And then it would suddenly start working again and the copies would be made.

Once, Barbel's GPS navigation system stopped working while we were on the way to an appointment. The entire radio console had died suddenly and wouldn't make so much as a peep, no matter which buttons she pressed. I remember telling her to just leave it alone, the fuse had probably gone and pressing buttons wouldn't help. 'Am I the creator of my world, or aren't I? I would like the GPS system to start working again,' she announced, and she closed her eyes and apparently talked the thing through with the cosmos. Shortly afterwards the radio gave a loud and abrupt 'click' and then both the radio and GPS system came back to life again. You had to have been there to believe it!

I just asked myself why she didn't manage to do the same thing recently with the washing machine – the repair bill turned out to be awfully expensive.

You clearly don't manage every time to focus your consciousness in such a way that even technical devices follow its lead, but there is a connection.

You don't think so? Come on, be honest, the more stress you are under, the more often the computer crashes. The more stupid I find my computer, the slower it becomes. Once again, an external 'problem' is just a reflection of my internal world! Even for my car, which won't start and keeps breaking down. Even for the washing machine and the video camera. When the computer goes on strike, what is it inside you that is refusing to work? When you have an accident and dent your car, what is it inside you that is dented and twisted? Just take a look at all of the things my consciousness can do; it can make computers break down – and repair them again. This brings us back to the ancient Hawaiians again. They believed that everything is suffused in thought: the machine I use, even the apples I eat. If I send them bad thoughts, then I really turn them bad, unhealthy or break them. We give souls to things through our consciousness. What is important is the conscious knowledge in which I do something. Our consciousness doesn't only notice things – it is downright able to *create* through the very act of noticing, thinking and feeling. This is why the copier goes on strike, then starts to work again. The hopp-technique in this case is *I love the part of me that caused the copier to go on strike.*

Sometimes it only wants a maintenance check and new toner – go ahead and treat it. But if the toner is new and everything else is in order, yet it still refuses to work, then it has to be down to you.

I see, so I can break the copier and repair it again simply through the power of my thoughts. So what about my own body? What consciousness do I give to my own cells and organs? How do I think about my own body? This bit is too fat, that bit too ugly, this bit is just not good enough. I've lost a bit of hair here, have too much hair there. (By the way, I find the rising number of cosmetic surgery operations very worrying, so I also hopp that *I love the part of me that ensures that so many operations are carried out in the pursuit of physical beauty.*)

Imagine I am a cell in my body and all I ever get to hear is, *You are so ugly, I don't like you.* That isn't very nice, is it? No wonder it makes me feel sick.

It is much better to think, *I love my body, I am thankful for my body. I forgive the little rolls of fat that make me look chubby. I completely accept my weight and my wrinkles.*

# COSMIC ORDERING AND HOPPING

*All things are ready*
*if our minds be so.*
**SHAKESPEARE**

When we start using wish-fulfilment techniques such as cosmic ordering or similar techniques, we usually want to achieve, or have, something very specific; we imagine we will only be able to be happy once it has been delivered. We wonder, then, when only little things are delivered and the large ones are not.

The truth is difficult to comprehend; the strongest force for changing our reality grows out of an acceptance of things as they are, and the decision to be happy with them as they are. The happy person is in maximum harmony with their creative power, the unhappy person is less so.

Yes, you need to let it sink in – you can be happy even if not all your wishes have been fulfilled.

First be happy, then the order will be delivered – it's a bitter pill to swallow.

The collected techniques around Ho'oponopono help us to internalize this and, in essence, increasingly to understand the soul better.

We notice, through regular use of all of these techniques, that when we give up our resistance to things as they are:

*What a relief to feel empathy rather than anger!*
*What a blessing when fears are transformed and you understand the pain of the person opposite.*
*What a gift to experience how much stronger and clearer our aura becomes when we are increasingly able to enfold obstacles peacefully into our heart.*
*How wonderful to be in the flow of life, instead of constantly resisting it.*

Let's have a look at the typical five phases of ordering and how you can move more rapidly to each new level by hopping.

*'I have a fundamental mistrust of life. Everything is awful, it is more than anybody can endure. I have to order everything to be different.'*

You have entered this phase because you are in a state of deep separation, separated from the cosmos and yourself. When you are in this state, everything has to go wrong; it is a kind of cosmic alarm bell, which is trying to steer your attention back towards yourself and inwards. In my (Barbel's) case, it had to ring the bell long and loud before I even noticed anything...

Just imagine that this is when you start hopping, using one technique after the other. Simply playing around with the double empathy technique with a small group of friends makes you begin to feel increasingly connected again: first with the others in the group, but then also with the universe. You notice this at the very latest when the anger and stress gradually fade and you become much calmer.

The first orders begin to be delivered. Thank heavens! Things are looking up and there is hope. You feel relieved and the feeling of complete separation from everything begins to ebb away: there is clearly 'someone' listening who is also able to intervene and shape your life according to your wishes. The strangest coincidences and successes in ordering occur and strokes of luck become ever more frequent.

Ho'oponopono quickly makes you realize, at this next stage, how little a coincidence usually has to do with chance: it is much more that it reflects your current mood and aura. Anyone who is stressed, introspective and full of angry thoughts overlooks opportunities that happen to chance by. But Ho'oponopono leads to you becoming more trusting and opening yourself up to the world again. And you suddenly find that you notice more wonderful opportunities for yourself.

So this really works, then? Well, in that case I'll order myself this first, and then that… We can usually think of a great many things we need in this phase – how much there is to order! And then we tweak and refine the technique to constantly improve the results. But after a while we also notice after the first flush of success that the deliveries begin to decrease in number again if we approach the issue too obsessively, whenever we feel that we absolutely have to have a certain order fulfilled.

*'I take the part that is becoming obsessive and greedy completely into my heart and I love myself in spite of it.'*

Hopp all the feelings that surface and take them into your heart, and soon you will be able to laugh about yourself instead of putting yourself under pressure.

We realize that gigantic miracles around us can occur, many things are delivered and we become closer to ourselves and to our inner voice. In this third phase we also increasingly feel how everything is connected to everything and everyone else. We become aware that we can affect others simply through the purity of our being, and begin to feel more responsible for what we encounter externally instead of seeing ourselves as a victim of fate. This is the essence of true liberation.

However, reality stubbornly refuses to let us take complete control of it. Everything has its limits – and this is a good thing, as we will see:

- This limit has something to do with supposed mistakes, which in fact aren't mistakes at all, as without them no life would be possible.

- It is also connected to Ho'oponopono, with unconditional self-love and self-forgiveness, as the Hawaiians had already discovered thousands of years ago.

- The fact is that on the other side of the curtain not every energy flow is moulded by truthfulness, and purity plays a similarly important role. Quite the opposite: only when our hearts are open and our intentions are pure are the answers from the cosmic consciousness equally pure. Otherwise conceit and intuition can easily be confused.

- It also has to do with the fact that we are forever connected to the entire cosmos and even possess a subatomic navigation system, as we have seen. Yet access to this is blocked, partly through our rationality, partly culturally and partly by the cosmic universal plan, so that even advanced cosmic orderers will need to carry out a few excavation exercises in order to fully return to the flow of being once again.

- And it has to do with the fact that we love *becoming* something instead of, above all, *being* something, as being is much more strenuous than becoming!

All of the Ho'oponopono techniques can also help you in this phase to enjoy the happiness you have and to feel thankful for everything. Ho'oponopono means that you view the glass as being half full instead of half empty.

Let's assume that you stayed stubbornly on the ball in phase four and more or less exactly achieved all of your larger goals. You have chosen the path towards happiness and all of a sudden everything increasingly seemed to be going your way.

What then follows seems to be unavoidable for every normal person: you wish that everything were even more beautiful, even bigger, even better, even more valuable. Nothing is worse than not having any goals left. But if you have arrived at this point in life through cosmic wish fulfilment, then the cosmos will speak up at this point, at the very latest. It will demand depth and more quality, rather than only 'higher, faster, more beautiful, more everything'. And it will speak clearly. When you have arrived at this point in life, then the universe will have a lot of possible methods of getting in contact with you and will communicate its desire for quality in many ways. At this stage of ordering, the universe wants to be fully connected to you again and to reveal itself in its absolute beauty and variety to you. This is only possible if you completely trust in the flow of life and trust in the fact that, ultimately, everything is in your very best interest. When you understand that miracles happen all by themselves as long as you maintain this internal connection, then you have reached the point at which you are ready to let go of concrete wishes, either partially or even completely. This doesn't mean that you should become a saint and never have any more desires. You can still order your lost shoelaces to reappear, just as you used to do in the past, instead of wasting hours searching for them. You can also order yourself new customers, perfect suppliers and a cosmic tip on where to find the best massage in town – or whatever you like.

What is meant is that you remain receptive and open to surprises and that instead of concrete events you prefer to order qualities and desirable feelings (for example, that you feel energetic, joyful, connected, in love, wise, awake, conscious, etc.) This gives the universe far more possibilities for delivery. And, apart from that, you will have much more fun because you will be surprised more often and the whole world will seem like one big miracle to you, in which everything is connected and interwoven.

One example of phase five ordering is our hedgehog order. It was only something small, but it is a good example as the deliveries were much better in the end than if everything had gone according to plan.

We had found an advert in a catalogue for a so-called hedgehog 'Hotel Ritz' and a hedgehog spiral. They were both hedgehog dens made out of ceramic and fireclay. They were waterproof, frostproof and the ideal comfortable shelter for the endangered hedgehog. I absolutely wanted to buy one to put in our garden, but didn't get around to it for ages. Being in the flow of life's energy, however, means not doing anything in a stressful or forced way, but rather to trust that you will remember to do whatever you need to do in time, and that this will be the best possible time to do it.

So eventually I found the time to order one. We set it up in the garden and the children helped me to cover it up with earth and branches. Now they naturally wanted to see a hedgehog appear as soon as possible…

This is exactly what I mean by the right point in time: while our little hedgehog house was still waiting to be occupied, we all travelled to Stuttgart for a lecture. We stayed overnight at a good friend of Manfred's. To our children's great joy, she confided in them that at 8 p.m. every evening they could watch hedgehog TV. But instead of turning on the television, she laid blankets and cushions on the living-room floor behind the open door to the terrace. We made ourselves comfortable and settled down to watch as an entire family of hedgehogs tucked into the food that she put out for them every evening. The children lay there for almost an entire hour, watching the hedgehogs and squeaking with delight.

In the meantime, we also have a hedgehog at home, but he has the habit of waiting until around midnight to eat. This is too late for the children, of course, so I wanted at least to take a picture of him to show them. This didn't pose any problem either. I simply followed my inner impulses. One night I woke up at 1.30 in the morning and wondered why I couldn't fall asleep again. After a while I got up, suddenly remembered our hedgehog, picked up the camera and went outside. I could already hear the little animal gobbling away as I crept towards it through the garden.

This kind of thing only works, of course, if you are at least a bit open to such inner impulses, recognize them and then also follow up on them.

This is where hopping comes in as an advanced turbo-boost technique. In a fantastic and light way, you train and fine-tune your sensibilities to your own inner impulses and feelings. You think that you are feeling your way into completely foreign situations: *If I were to act like that, why would I do so?* You don't get the feeling that you are putting a lot of effort into working on yourself, and yet you can only ever find yourself, whatever problem you examine. The more people you allow to take part, the more varied the results you will get. Each person always only discovers a different part within themselves. Each person comes a little closer to understanding themselves every time they do an exercise, and so gets closer to the cosmic truth about themselves: being in harmony with the whole.

Sooner or later we finally throw the satellite navigation system out of the window when we are completely reconnected with ourselves, because we 'hear' our subatomic navigation system telling us which way to go as soon as a new intention forms within us – consciously or not.

On this note, we wish you happy hopping and successful ordering.

Barbel and Manfred

P.S. As always, we hope you find this book inspirational and don't view it as a lecture. We understand that it is a fact of nature that all people are different and that the images they carry within them are sometimes closer to, sometimes further from, reality, and that maybe some will be able to make use of parts of what we have written and some perhaps nothing at all. This is not a problem in any way – anyone who objects will simply be 'hopped over'.

(But we know that this is clearly impossible, don't we? Since we can only hopp parts of ourselves, the most we can do is to hopp on our own objections.)

And if you think that what we have written is rubbish, then why don't you hopp us, we'll hopp you, we'll all hopp each other and we will keep going until the whole world feels reconnected in cosmic unity because we have re-established the harmony within ourselves. We wish you all

LOVE, PEACE & HARMONY.

# SUMMARY OF THE EMPATHY TECHNIQUE

- Choose a person (a neighbour, relative, partner, friend, colleague – male or female…) or a situation that is causing you problems.

- The reason why the other person is behaving that way is not your problem! But you can heal the resonance to it within yourself.

- Ask yourself, *If I were to act like this (like your colleague, etc.) why would I do so? How would I feel in doing so?*

- If you discover a feeling *inside yourself,* say *to yourself: I am sorry, I love me!*

Important note: the reason why the other person is behaving like this is still completely irrelevant. You can only heal your own resonance to it by asking yourself what *your* motive for such behaviour would be. You heal this motive in yourself, *not* in the other person. The other person can take care of themselves!

This exercise causes two things to happen:

- The understanding grows within you that it is possible to act in this way through your own internal problems. You begin to see the behaviour of others no longer as an attack upon yourself, but rather as an expression of the problems and pain they are experiencing in their lives. As soon as you can experience this through these exercises, *you are free!* You will inevitably be freer and happier, whatever the other person does.

- The change in your resonance very often leads, in the long run (and sometimes also immediately, as we have seen from the examples), to the other person changing their behaviour towards you, without you having to say a word. Their old behaviour simply no longer fits your resonance. The other person can change the moment that *your* happiness no longer depends on *their* behaviour!

In step two you can ask yourself why you have created such a situation for yourself and then also heal the resulting feeling with an 'I love me' and so on.

End each exercise by expressing your thanks: *Thank you, thank you, thank you!* Give thanks for the insight you have gained, thanks for the feelings and thanks for the love.

.

# ABOUT THE AUTHOR

Bestselling author **Barbel Mohr** is a household name in Germany and travelled all over the world teaching transformational workshops on Cosmic Ordering until her death in 2010. Barbel first wrote *The Cosmic Ordering Service* for a small group of friends and distributed it as photocopies until its popularity prompted her to publish it.

She went on to write a whole series of powerful books that have helped countless people to change their lives for the better. Barbel's husband, Manfred Huerth, continues to promote her work and its empowering message internationally.

Barbel is also the author of *Cosmic Ordering for Beginners*, *Instant Cosmic Ordering* and *21 Golden Rules for Cosmic Ordering*.

www.baerbelmohr.de

# HAY HOUSE

*Look within*

Join the conversation about latest products,
events, exclusive offers and more.

 Hay House UK

 @HayHouseUK

 @hayhouseuk

 healyourlife.com

*We'd love to hear from you!*

26930326R00104

Printed in Great Britain
by Amazon